Form and Will Boxing
XINGYIQUAN *(Shing Yee Chuan)*

Sugawara Martial Arts / Japan Publications

Chinese Martial Arts Series
FORM AND WILL BOXING *(Xingyiquan)*
- One of the Big Three Internal Chinese Body Boxing Styles
ISBN: 0-87040-942-5
Written and Performed by Lin Jianhua
Translated by Mei Xuexiong (Associate professor of Fujian Teachers'
University, China)
Photograph Editor: Xing Yanling, Xing Lujian

Published by Sugawara Martial Arts Institute, Inc.
20-13, Tadao 3 chome, Machida-shi, Tokyo 194 Japan.
Telephone: (0427) 94-0972 / FAX: (0427) 94-0899

Printed-out to the films: Access International Inc., Japan
Printing by Hosoya Printing Co.
Printed in Japan
First printing: March 1995

Distributor:
UNITED STATES: Kodansha America, Inc., through Farrar, Straus &
Giroux, 19 Union Square West, New York, NY 10003. CANADA:
Fitzhenry & Whiteside Ltd., 195 Allstate Parkway, Markham, Ontario L3R
4T8. BRITISH ISLES AND EUROPEAN CONTINENT: Premier Book
Marketing Ltd., 1 Gower Street, London WC1E 6HA. AUSTRALIA AND
NEW ZEALAND: Bookwise International, 54 Crittenden Road, Findon,
South Australia 5023. THE FAR EAST AND JAPAN: Japan Publications
Trading Co., Ltd., 1-2-1, Sarugaku-cho, Chiyoda-ku, Tokyo 101.

Form and Will Boxing
Xingyiquan (Shing Yee Ch'uan)

One of the Big Three Internal Chinese Body Boxing Styles

by Lin Jianhua

Sugawara Martial Arts / Japan Publications

About my teacher, Wen Jingming (1905-1985),

Chinese most excellent educationist in martial arts, Vice Chairman of China Wushu Association, Professor of Wuhan University of Physical Education, was proficient at all kinds of martial arts with a good and solid foundation. As a representative of Chinese Physical Training Delegation he joined the 11th Olympic Games held in Berlin, Germany in 1936. He gave an excellent performance which made a great sensation throughout games. He served as a chief judge and direction of the board of Arbitration many times during the national Wushu games.

Being engaged in Wushu education for sixty years, he educated and trained a great number of qualified Wushu people. He is hishly repeated and deeply loved by the people in China Wushu field.

Teacher, He Fusheng, and author

Xingyiquan training

Foreword

Wushu (Chinese martial arts) was a kind of self-defence arts for laboring people to survive in ancient China as well as a traditional way for people to keep fit. It is a crystallization of Chinese national wisdom and a valuable cultural heritage, and it has now enjoyed growing favor among people both at home and abroad.

As a child, I was very fond of Wushu and admired very much the smartness and nimbleness of those adults who were practising Wushu. In 1964, when I was 12 years old, I went to learn Wushu basic skills, 12 routines of Spring Leg etc. In 1973, I entered the Department of Physical Education of Fujian Normal University, majoring in Wushu, where I received strict and systematic training under the direction of Professor Guo Minghua, Professor Lin Jinde and Professor Hu Jinhuan.

On graduation from the university, I became a Wushu teacher in the Department of Physical Education of Fujian Normal University. In 1979, I went to Wuhan Institute of Physical Education to study martial arts in a national advanced class for university Wushu teachers, where I was fortunately taught by Professor Wen Jingming, the most famous Wushu educator, former vice-president of Wushu Association of China, and Professor Liu Yuhua. Professor Wen and Liu personally taught me Xingyiquan (Form and Will Boxing), Baguazhang (Eight-diagram Palm), Kaoshou-fanziquan and Liuhe-spearplay, which are excellent traditional Wushu routines. Professor Wen often encouraged us by saying: 'Be a successor and spreader of Wushu and make Wushu beneficial to our offspring and the whole mankind.' His words have been inspiring me deeply and will be in my mind forever.

While learning Xingyiquan from Professor Wen, I was deeply attracted by this marvellous martial art. I was fascinated by its plain and rigorous movements, its simple and vigorous exertion of strength, its unique technical style and its outstanding effects of both the internal and the external training. At that time, from early morning till late night, I spared no pains to exercise Xingyiquan, again and again, from the three-in-one posture to every form of the five-element boxing. My skill of Xingyiquan was quickly upgraded because Professor Wen and Professor Liu often stayed with me, correcting my movements and postures, helping me to improve my technique. On the ceremony of the course completion, specially asked by Professor Wen, I represented the class to perform Xingyiquan, and my performance received favourable appraisal.

Since then, I have practised Xingyiquan every day without interruption for more than fifteen years, and Xingyiquan has now become my good companion. During this period, I have luckily received direction from a number of well-known seniors of Xingyiquan, such as Professor Kang Shaoyuan, President of Wushu Association of Jilin; Mr. He Fusheng, President of Wushu Association of Yunnan; Professor Zhou Yongxiang of Jinan Normal University in Shandong; Mr. Wang Jingchun, a famous master of Xingyiquan from Henan; and Mr. Zhang Tong, a famous expert from Shanxi. From them I have learnt a lot of methods and have derived beneficial nourishment. This has influenced my style of Xingyiquan to a certain extent. However, my style of Xingyiquan remains basically that of Professor Wen Jingming, namely the style of Hebei School—extensive, grave and vigorous. Seeing my performance in 1989, Mr. He Fusheng, who and Professor Wen were classmates of the Central National Wushu College 60 years ago, said in surprise that my movements were very much similar to those of professor Wen.

Now, I have been teaching Wushu in universities for nearly 20 years and I have trained a great number of students some of whom from Europe, America and other Asian countries. Many members of foreign visiting groups have also attended my Wushu classes to learn Chinese martial arts including Xingyiquan. It is a pleasure to see that these foreign students are as enthusiastic as Chinese students. I deeply esteem them for their keenness on Wushu and their assiduousness in exercise. Through learning Wushu, they have learnt more about traditional Chinese culture and have strengthened the friendship with Chinese people. Jakob Sonnenberg, a Danish youth, has twice to Amoy to learn Wushu from me, and he once said: 'Chinese martial arts is one of the greatest sports in the world and I like Xingyiquan best.'

At the end of 1992, I received a letter from my friend Ms. Xing Yanling, who was a Wushu coach at Fujian College of Traditional Chinese Medicine and is now teaching Wushu in Japan. She told me that she would like to publish a book on Xingyiquan, introducing this excellent martial art to the world, and she would expect such a book from me. I was very pleased to accept this significant proposal. In June 1993, Xing came to China with a visiting group led by Mr. Tetsutaka Sugawara, the director of Sugawara Martial Arts Institute, Aikido 6th Dan. They spent two days taking pictures of my performance of Xingyiquan.

After one and a half year of efforts, this book, Form and Will Boxing—one of the Big three Chinese Internal Body Boxing styles, is now about to go to press. At this time, I am specially missing Professor Wen

Jingming and Professor Liu Yuhua, who have brought me into the gate of Xingyiquan.

I would like to express my gratitude to the many Wushu teachers who have given me guidance and to all the friends who have helped in any way to accomplish this book. I am specially grateful to Mr. Tetsutaka Sugawara, who has made great efforts to spread Chinese martial arts and publish this book; to Professor Mei Xuexiong of Fujian Normal University, who, in the midst of his pressing affairs, has done a remarkable job to translate the draft of this book into English; and to my beloved tutor, Professor Lin Jinde, who has written the preface to this book. I am also deeply indebted to Mr. Xing Lujian, who has offered great energies to develop all the pictures for this book. My hearty thanks also extend to Mr. Zhang Guocai of Amoy University, and to my students Chen Hua, Su Jianhui, Wang Yong, Lin Dezhi and Jakob who have aided in taking pictures of the paired practice.

My sincere thanks are also due to Ms. Xing Yanling, who has spent much time and has made great efforts to facilitate the publication of this book. Without her initiative, this book could not be drought into being.

To conclude, I wish to express my heartfelt thanks to my dear wife Wu Shuiying, who returned from U.S.A. not long ago. In order to provide a favorable environment so that I could concentrate on writing this book, she has taken on almost all the household chores after her business.

Lin Jianhua
Amoy University
Amoy, Fujian
 Province
China
October 5, 1994

VII

Preface

Xingyiquan (Form and Will Boxing) is one of the main schools of traditional Chinese martial arts and is among those that have the longest history and the greatest influence. Based on the ancient Oriental philosophy of Yin-Yang, this boxing, mimicking and taking meaning from the behavior of some kinds of animals, places special stress on the high integration of external form and internal will of mind. It has therefore been so named as "Form and Will Boxing". For hundreds of years, Xingyiquan has won widespread acclaim as an effective self-defence skill. People like it still much because of its special function to build up health and develop strength. Its features such as being clear about motion and rest, having hardness and softness promoting each other, moving with great speed sometimes and at a leisurely pace sometimes and combining the appearance and the spirit into one are noticeable.

Mr. Lin Jianhua, keen on martial arts from his childhood, graduated from the physical Education Department of Fujian Normal University in 1976, majoring in martial arts. After graduation, he has visited many famous masters and learns a lot from them. Being versatile and in the prime of life, he is now a martial arts teacher at Amoy University, a council member of the Fujian Martial Arts Association, the vice-president of the Amoy Martial Arts Association and the president of Martial Arts Association of Amoy University. He has published a number of articles on martial arts and a book entitled "The Prevailing Martial Arts in the World" which has won favorable appraisal in the martial arts circle. Owing to his talent and excellent teaching accomplishment, he was invited by the Ateneo de Manila University of the Phillipines to give lectures on Chinese martial arts in 1990, and he was highly appreciated. For the past decade, Mr. Lin has studied diligently and trained hard. He has made thorough investigations and systematic researches on the Xingyiquans prevailing in various districts and possessing different technical features, and he has formed some original views of his own. He has become a mature expert of Xingyiquan.

Form and Will Boxing, written by Mr. Lin Jianhua, systematically introduces the rationale and methods of Xingyiquan. It not only carries forward the traditions, but also gives scientific expositions, making the book full of novel lights. This book, rich in content, is elaborately compiled, with the routines carefully chose and practically arranged, the clear pictures accompanied by plain and vivid explanations.

I am willing to recommend this book to the lovers and researchers of Xingyiquan both at home and abroad. For beginners of Xingyiquan, it deserves to called a qualified guide. Having a copy in hand, one is able to teach oneself. As it is a comprehensive summary of Xingyiquan knowledge as well as a fruit of research on Chinese martial arts, it may after all be accepted as a worthful reference for specialists. I am sure that the publication of this book will contribute to a wider and further study of Xingyiquan all over the world and promote the international cultural exchange.

Lin Jinde
Professr of P. E. Dept.
Fujian Normal University
Fuzhou, Fujian Province
P. R. China
October 5, 1994

Preface

Before and after my graduation from college, I often got advice in Chinese martial arts from Mr. Lin Jianhua. Over the years, I have met with many martial arts teachers and received instructions from many martial experts of various boxing branches. I feel that Mr. Lin Jianhua is proficient in many kinds of boxing, especially of great attainment in Xingyiquan. He has spent much time and energy in Learning from famous masters of Xingyiquan of today, accumulating a great amount of information, and making thorough researches on theories and methods of every branches of Xingyiquan. Through many years' painstaking labour, absorbing the quintessences of all schools of Xingyiquan, he has evolved a style of his own.

Mr. Lin Jianhua's brilliant attainments were the cause of my suggestion that he write a book to introduce Xingyiquan. I am sure that this book will give the readers a comprehensive understanding of Xingyiquan and furthermore a better understanding of traditional Chinese culture, and I hope that this book can serve as a cultural bridge to link up enthusiasts of martial arts all over the world.

Xing Yanling
    in Tokyo

First Class Judge of Chinese Martial Arts
Former Coach of Fujian Institute of Traditional Chinese Medicine
Coach of Sugawara Martial Arts Institute, Japan
Guest Instructor of Shanghai Institute of Physical Education
January 31, 1995

The author and the staff when taking photographs in Fujian Province in China.

Contents

Chapter Five : Shadowboxing Routines 113

Chapter Six : Paired Practice 161

Chapter One
Introduction

Xingyiquan (*Shing-Yee-Ch'uan* or Form and Will Boxing) is one of the main schools of traditional Chinese martial arts, and it lays stress on improving man's internal elements such as spirit, vital energy, awareness and strength. Just as the Chinese term suggests, Xingyiquan is a kind of boxing with external form and internal spirit highly-integrated, or an art of imitation and understanding. "It can not be a kind of boxing with only internality but without externality, and it can not be an art with only externality but without internality." Here, the internality means the way to keep in good health, and the externality is the skill of exercise. Through practising Xingyiquan, with the body base enhanced and the inner solidified, one can build up his health, strengthen his physique, defend himself from harm, as well as cultivate his character, temper his will-power, mould his temperament and foster his lofty sentiment.

1. The Origin and the Development of Xingyiquan

Xingyiquan was originally called "Mind and Will Boxing", "Jike Boxing." During its development, it has gotten some other aliases such as "Mind and Will Boxing of Six Conformities". The present name is the latest formal one.

There are three legends about the origin of Xingyiquan. One of these legends explained that Xingyiquan was created by Damo, an eminent Indian monk, who came to China to disseminate Buddhism in A.D. 520. Another story tells that Yue Fei (A.D.1103-1141), a famous general of the Northern Song Dynasty, selected the essence of spearplay in which he was especially skilled and worked out the miraculous boxing to train his military men. However, through researches, Wushu (martial arts) historians hold that Damo was no good at martial arts, therefore he had nothing to do with Xingyiquan. Likewise, strong evidence that can confirm Yue Fei's making of this boxing is still wanting.

According to the historical materials now available, Xingyiquan was created by Ji Jike, a villager of Yongjizun, Shanxi Province. Ji Jike, styled Longfeng, was born in the period of Wanli of Ming Dynasty, and died at his eighties in the early years of Kangxi of Qing Dynasty. What with his keenness on martial arts in his youth and his intelligence and assiduousness, he became an expert in this realm. The Ji's Family Tree said that Jike was extremely skilled in martial arts. Having a large following, he was once called a superspear.

At his middle ages, Ji Jike had lived in Shaolin Temple in Mount Songshan for a decade. The monks there greatly appreciated his boxing skill, and he also gained a good deal of enlightenment from the Shaolin boxing. One day while he was reading a book in the temple, he was fascinated by two cocks locked in fighting, and he gradually realized why it should be so. From then on, he devoted himself to the study of habits and characteristics of various animals. In the end, with reference to the Shaolin boxing of dragon, tiger, leopard, snake and crane styles then in vogue, he worked out a brand-new school of boxing called "Mind and Will Boxing of Six Conformities." After returning home, Ji Jike imported this boxing widespreadly. People venerated him for his moral character and martial power and hence named the boxing "Jike Boxing."

From the times of Qianlong of Qing Dynasty, Xingyiquan spread far and wide in the vicinity of Shanxi, Henan and Hebei. Dai Longban and Ma Xueli studied martial arts under Cao Jiwu, a disciple of Ji Jike, and they got the true essence of Xingyiquan. Afterward, Dai Longban passed on this boxing to many people including Li Feiyu who, through assiduous training, became accomplished in martial arts and was regarded as the outstanding master of the day. Li Feiyu then returned to Hebei to spread Xingyiquan. It was said that he had the greatest number of students some of whom were also of high reputation in the history. Another development was initiated by Ma Xueli in Henan. He was also successful in bringing up a group of brilliant masters of Xingyiquan.

Through three hundreds' evolution and development, with the constant practice of thousands of people, both the technique and the theory of Xingyiquan have greatly been improved. However, owing to the environment and modification made by pugilists of different districts, some styles that differ from each other have been shaped. The Xingyiquan in Shanxi is noted for the well-knit movements and the ingenious strength exertion; the Xingyiquan in Henan has the unique features of vigorous motion and tremendous momentum; as the Xingyiquan in Hebei distinguishes itself with its expansive posture and the simple and steady manner. In spite of these, we can still think of Xingyiquan as having two main branches, the southern one prevailing in Henan, the northern one popular in Shanxi and Hebei.

In recent years, Xingyiquan has made its way more widespreadly. Its excellent health-building value and its practical effect of attack-defence have been recognized by more and more people. We can notice its prevalence at home and find its flourish in the United States of America, Canada, Japan and Southern Asia as well.

2. The Main Characteristics of Xingyiquan

Xingyiquan is good for practising both the internal and the external. It can also be called a kind of boxing of imitation and understanding because it follows some animals' patterns of action and senses the meaning. For instance, the twelve-animal style boxing is just modeled on the typical features of dragon, tiger, monkey, horse, alligator, cock, sparrow hawk, swallow, snake, "tai", eagle and bear. The

boldness and valour of a tiger springing on its prey, the nimbleness and dexterousness of a monkey climbing a pole, the tremendous momentum of a horse galloping ahead, the accuracy of a cock pecking at the rice, the skillfulness of a swallow skimming over the water and so forth are vividly manifested through the movements. However, the movements are completely designed in the light of health-building theories and attack-defence principles. The main characteristics of Xingyiquan are as follows:

1) Simple and Clear

The basic movements of Xingyiquan are simple and clear without a trace of gaudiness, putting stress on straight moves of fists and feet. For instance, the five methods of the five-element boxing look uncomplicated, but they really contain much subtlety. We must practise constantly to fulfill the different requirements of the methods, so that we can come up to a high level of integrity of strength and a complete combination of the inside and the outside, thus see ingenuousness in common-place and seek after the true essence in plainness. This is in keeping with the attack-defence principles of Xingyiquan which favour the quick and straight offensive and advocate to gain the initiative by striking first. It is often said that "An inch more, a gain of advantage", "Once you make a move, you hit the enemy." So no showiness but practicality is needed.

2) Compact and Well-organized

While practising Xingyiquan, you should coordinate your limbs and trunk, giving an expression of compactness. The repeated and crisscross rising, falling, penetrating and overturning of the arms should be carried out with twisting, wrapping, embracing and spiral strength. In many cases, when one arm extends, the other bends; when one arm goes up, the other drops. In fist-thrusting, you have to safeguard your heart with your hands and protect your ribs with your elbows. Be sure not to spread elbows sideward. As a Wushu (martial arts) jargon indicates, "You should move arms close against the body, with hands not far from the heart and elbows not far from the ribs." You must not, in the slightest degree, slack off with hand attack, but be prepared constantly. "The thrusting hand is like a steel file, and the withdrawing hand is like a pole with a hook at the end." Likewise, while taking steps, you should close your crotch, bend the knee and properly turn the toes in so as to be quick and steady. In turning round, you must act swiftly, using the waist as the axis. The whole body is just like a tightly-twisted rope full of tenacity and resilience.

3) Steady and Composed

While practising Xingyiquan, you should take firm stances, step steadily, expand your breast, solidify your abdomen and lead the energy stream down to "dantian (lower abdomen)". You should manage to keep your shoulders lowered, elbows dropped, waist down and hips in. As an old saying goes: "Step as if you were ploughing the field, and put your foot down as if it took root." The aim is to attain an extended upper body and stable lower limbs. The movements should be neither loose nor stiff, engendering a feeling of ease and solemnity. Having a smooth outside and a substantial inside, your whole body will be imbued with great vigor.

4) Harmonious and Integrated

Harmony of movements and integration of strength are important for practising with Xingyiquan. Once a will comes forth, the hands, feet, trunk and the line of vision should reach their proper positions at the same time. The strength should be concentrated on a particular target accurately. When you carry out a move, the tips of the middle finger, the nose and the foot should be kept in a same vertical plane. Talking of arm action, the force should be exerted from the shoulders, transmitted to the elbows, and brought to the hands. Likewise, with regard to leg movements, the force should be exerted from the hips, transmitted to the knees, and brought to the feet. All parts of the body should be linked up smoothly in a right process. The mind guides the energy stream, and the energy stream promotes the strength. No section is at a standstill while any part is in motion. As a verse goes: "First and foremost you should press close to the opponent at grips, yet your move would come to nothing without a coordination of hands and feet." This not only shows a method of attack, but also manifests the unison and integrity of the body as a whole. You should bear in mind that harmony of the body leads to integrated strength.

3. The Attack-defence Features of Xingyiquan

Xingyiquan is held in high esteem in the world of martial arts for its simple and unadorned movements. It is also famous for its traits of hand-to-hand fight and quick and straight offensive. No move is not designed for actual combat. Strategically, you should despise your enemy, having the courage and resourcefulness to face danger fearlessly and advance bravely. You should dare to struggle and dare to win. This spirit of dauntlessness is repeatedly emphasized in various words: "Take the initiative in launching offensive and do not assume passive defensive so long as there is still a gleam of chance", "Strike as if walking, and look upon the enemy just as weeds", "Practise as if you encountered an actual opponent, and get into combat as if the opponent did not exist."

Tactically, Xingyiquan stresses mobile and changeable moves. You can defeat your opponent either by taking the initiative in launching the offensive, or by attacking only after the opponent has struck the blow but hitting him before his blow reaches you. Be motionless like a stone, or be vigorous like a tiger. It is important to occupy a superior position in a fight. "Step in the middle to control the commanding point, even the celestial being can not avoid the strike." Every part of the body should cooperate harmoniously to exert great power in a flash so as to knock out the enemy before he recognizes what the blow is.

Xingyiquan is particular about fighting a quick battle and forcing a quick decision. You make no delay and show no mercy once the combat begins. You must act swiftly, violently, straightforwardly and efficiently, leaving your opponent no way of withstanding. Wushu veterans usually describe this feature in picturesque terms some of which are as follows: "Start off like an arrow, and drop like a wind." "Ride the wind to chase after the moon without a shred of slackness." "Be quick of eye and deft of hand, eager to struggle and confident of success." "Leap like a fierce tiger springing on its prey, and dive like a vigorous goshawk pursuing a hare." "Launch an attack like a flash of lightning, strike the enemy like a sudden peal of thunder."

In a combat, you have to use your head, shoulders, elbows, hands, hips, knees and feet freely and effectively in the light of specific conditions. Your head can be used to knock the opponent at the face, bridge of nose, temples or breast. Your shoulders can be applied to give the opponent a front or back bump. Your elbows can be wielded up and down, to the side or in the middle, to confuse the opponent and strike him. The moves of the hands are more unpredictable and efficient. You never raise, lower, overturn or stretch your hands without a definite purpose. You must carry out hand-moves like a tiger springing on a lamb. If the opponent attacks from the left side, you must uphold your left arm to parry the blow and thrust your right fist to beat him, and vice versa. You can use your hands or feet to deal with the opponent in a distance, but employ your elbows and knees to subdue the opponent if he is much closer to your body. Any section of the body can be applied at any time for purpose of driving the opponent into such a holpless position as being unable to stand up to your varied and fast-changing blows.

4. Requirements and Steps of Practice

Xingyiquan requires that all parts of the body be well coordinated. The hand technique stresses hardness with softness residing in it. You should express yourself in a manner of showing concentrated attention through your eyes. The bodywork must be integrated and the footwork be swift and steady. You should perform in clear rhythm, alternate skillfully between motion and stationariness, and manage to reach a close combination of the mind and the body. To come up to a high standard, you should practise step by step in a planned way which was indicated by predecessors as "three stages."

1) The First Stage

The first aims at a solid foundation, in other words, the formation of "clear strength." In this stage, importance should be attached to developing your strength, fortifying your body, and cultivating majestic making. You should take steps swiftly and steadily, conduct the rising, dropping, stretching and overturning of the hands at high speed and with twisting force. Although you must shun waviness and slackness in practise, clear strength does not mean rigidity, strain or inflexibility, but smooth movements and natural breathing. Speaking in concrete terms, the following requirements must be fulfilled:

a) **Correct Positions:**
The correct body positions in Xingyiquan

are: head upright, neck erect, shoulders lowered, chest naturally drawn in, back extended, waist down, hips held in, torso straight, palm out-expanded and fist clenched tight. Beginners have to start from a basic exercise called "three-in-one posture" to master the correct positions and establish a solid foundation for technical improvement. Be sure not to be careless with any movement in this stage. Having grasped the essentials of the three-in-one posture, you may exercise in Chop Palm first in fixed stance and then in free steps, and progressively proceed to practise the Five-element Boxing and others.

b) Integration of Movements:

While practising Xingyiquan, you must integrate all your movements into one. In particular, your arms and legs should be well coordinated, no matter which hand you thrust out and which foot you set in front. The step, as well as the fist-thrusting, and the exertion of strength must synchronize perfectly. You should strive to reach the integration of hands and feet, of elbows and knees, and of shoulders and hips. As a Wushu (Martial arts) jargon goes: "A coordination of hands with feet embodies genuineness." This is a precondition for a good command of Xingyiquan, for you could arrive at an overall integration only if you first met the coordination of limbs.

c) Smoothness of Advance and Retreat:

Smooth advance and retreat can help you perform harmoniously, steadily, freely and naturally. For instance, if your front foot is turned too far inward or outward while you are practising the cannon fist, you are inevitably out of balance because of the unduly strained muscles. If you hold your arm too high or do not well round it while carrying out some moves, you are bound to incline or shrug your shoulders. Besides, ragged movements of arms or legs will unavoidably result in hard breathing. It is just what the saying "without smoothness outside, there would be no conformity inside" means. Therefore, beginners should pay great attention to the basic training for smooth action, harmony of upper and lower body, clear distinction between solidity and emptiness, and formation of a straight standing.

d) Balance and Steadiness:

Balance and steadiness are inseparable from correct positions and smoothness of advance and retreat. When you begin to learn "Five-element Boxing", you should try to keep good balance. Never can you incline forward or lean backward, or rise one movement and drop the next, whether you are advancing, retreating or turning round. While stepping, you should move your foot close to the ground as if you were ploughing the fields. Although the movements of the "Twelve-animal Style Boxing" are more complicated, you should still move as fast as a wind and stand as firm as a nail. In order to improve your ability to maintain good balance and stability, you are required to take conscious activities to strengthen your legs. In point of this, the three-in-one posture is particularly worthy of application.

e) Being Powerful:

When you begin to learn Xingyiquan, you should clench fists tight and manage to exert strength as clear as possible. This preliminary requirement aims at the integration of head, hands and feet as well as will, vital energy and strength, and it is just what the saying "strengthen the body to fortify the foundation" indicates. The better the parts of the body coordinate, the more powerful you will be. Take the "Punch Fist in Forward Step" for instance, your front foot should go as far as possible with the sole close to the ground, and your rear foot should assist the advance with a powerful drive. You should synchronize the straightening of the rear leg, the twist of the torso, the forward push of the right shoulder, the withdrawal of the left fist with the thrust of the right fist, so as to produce a burst of impulsive force. Moreover, a coordination of breathing with movements can help increase strength. Usually you should inhale when you begin to accumulate strength, and exhale when you are exerting strength.

2) The Second Stage

In the second stage, you must strive to have your movements linked up more smoothly and perform more exquisitely. Speaking particularly, you ought to pay more attention to the training for better flexibility and pliability on the strength you have already achieved in order that you can effectively develop the special ability which Mr. Guo Yunshen called "latent strength." You have to limber up yourself so that the integrative strength can grow ceaselessly. Of the two kinds, clear strength is fiery and forthright, yet latent strength is relatively implicit and firm. You should strive to come up to such a standard as being able to act at high speed or at low speed, in high stances or in low stances, to dodge, extend, jump or move with both clear rhythm and flowing momentum. Your limbs must be as tough and tensile as an unbreakable steel bar whether you are thrusting with the fist or chopping with the palm. All the hand-moves, including parrying, wrapping, upward drilling, downward pressing, forward pushing and backward drawing, should be carried out tenaciously. The sound with your steps also becomes weaker in this stage. In this manner, the strength seems to diminish, but indeed it has changed from being exerted apparently into being stored inside. In other words, the nature of the strength is shifting from hardness to softness, from explicitness to implicitness. You can thus greatly mobilize all your muscles and improve the coordination and the integration of the body.

3) The Third Stage

The goal set for the third stage is to reach a high combination of consciousness and

movements, and a good concordance of internal spirit and external forms on what has been achieved during the former two periods. Then, you will be able to act with high proficiency and apply what Mr. Guo Yunshen addressed "neutralizing strength."

Neutralizing strength is such a capacity as controlling your opponent efficiently by following his to-and-fro movements, and it actually reflects the exquisite of the inner power and vital energy. This kind of strength can bring about magical effects, but you have to abandon your own intention so as to yield to your opponent's motion. See that you neither separate from nor make forcible contact with your opponent. Be hard while the opponent is soft, and be soft while the opponent becomes hard. To develop neutralizing strength, whether with advancing, retreating, rising, dropping, stretching, contracting, opening, overturning or changing from one form to another, you should act as spryly and nimbly as a cat or an ape. All your movements should be continuous like a current flowing smoothly and uninterruptedly.

In this stage, more stress should be laid on the aspect of spirit than on the apparent forms. You should make greater efforts to manifest the "six conformities of the internal and external" and the "combination of will and form" in the transformation of motion and stationariness, of hardness and softness, and of solidity and emptiness.

1

Chapter Two
Essentials

Over more than three centuries of development, a comprehensive technical and theoretical system of Xingyiquan has taken shape. The great masters of the ages have put forward many original views on Xingyiquan and have left many brilliant expositions. To study the theory of Xingyiquan would be a great help to practitioners who want to have a better grasp of the technique. As a saying goes: "Without a good understanding of the theory, the skill is inevitably under consummation." Therefore, beginners ought to make a serious study of the theory as well as practise the movements with assiduity.

1. Three Sections

According to the theory of Xingyiquan, the whole body or a particular segment of the body can be divided into three sections. Talking of the body as a whole, the head is the upper section (the tip section), the trunk is the middle section, and the legs are the lower section (the base section). Of the head, the tip section refers to the part above the forehead, the middle section is the nose and the base section is the chin; whereas the three sections of the trunk refer respectively to the neck, the chest, and the belly. Likewise, the hands, the elbows and the shoulders make up the three sections of the upper limbs; the feet, the knees and the hips form the three sections of the lower limbs. And of the hand, the tip section, the middle section and the base section correspond respectively to the fingers, the palms and the bases of the palms. In a word, there is no part of the body that can not be divided into three sections. Just as the classics of Xingyiquan state: "Without the differentiation of three sections, you will be at a loss for what to focus your attention on. If you are not clear about your upper section, you will have nothing to depend on; and if you are not clear about your lower section, you are bound to tumble the moment you move." "Without a clear distinction among three sections, there is no skillful transformation of movements indeed." "You can not be effective enough to defeat your enemy if you fail to grasp the method of the three sections."

The significance of dividing one into three is for a better application of energy and strength. First, it refers to a right process of a movement: the tip section starts off, the middle section follows and the base section rouses to catch up. Taking the example of the "slap palm" or the "up-striking palm", the move should be completed with the palm going first, the elbow following immediately and the shoulder running after. Second, it refers to a correct sequence of strength exertion. The force of the tip section originates from the middle section, and the force of the middle sections comes out from the base section. In other words, the force should be exerted from the base section, immediately transmitted to the middle section, and finally brought to the tip section. As in the "punch fist", the force emerges from the shoulder, comes to the elbow, and then reaches the hand, or you can say, the legs (the base section) impulse the torso (the middle section), and the torso bring along the hands (the tip section). Only with the three sections linked up smoothly in a right process, can you exert the integrated strength with great efficiency.

2. Three Centres

The three centres refer to the hollows of the hands, the undersides of the arches of the feet and central part of the chest. "The three centres must be drawn in." That is to say, you ought to keep your hands and feet appropriately curved inward like a concave mirror and do not thrust your chest out. In this manner, you can accumulate strength still better and exert greater explosive force. The hands well cupped enable the arms to extend and withdraw freely, with the force transmitted smoothly to the finger. The feet perfectly arched can enhance the stamping force on the sole and toes, making your steps more steady and nimble. To keep the chest in is a profound requirement of Xingyiquan and it enables you to maintain an empty breast and a substantial abdomen by guiding the energy stream down to "dantian", thus helps you to keep constant balance like a tumbler. It also implies that you should concentrate your attention and keep calm so that you can deal with any emergency composedly.

There is still another way of saying the three centres: "The three centres must be solidified." This means that the centres of the hands, feet and chest should be full of energy at the moment you are launching an attack, so that you can exert your inner power explosively

3. The Three-in-one Posture

The three-in-one posture is one of the main stances of Xingyiquan, and the most important stake exercise as well. Through regular practice in this posture, you can not only strengthen your lower limbs to keep the torso erect, but also promote the circulation of vital energy and blood with respiration exercise, thus improve your health and build up a powerful physique. It is true that thousands of moves come from the three-in-one posture. From this we can see its significance.

The three-in-one posture is also called "bow-drawing posture" for the position of the body and the strength applied are very much like those required to bend a bow. Another name for it is "three-treasure posture." Here, the three treasures refer to the heaven, the earth and the human beings which, in the ancients' opinion, possess three other treasures each. The treasures of the heaven are the sun, the moon and the stars; the treasures of the earth means water, fire and wind; whereas those of the human beings refer to vigou, vital energy and spirit. All of these are considered as key factors determining the changes of the

nature and the life and death of a man. The term "three-in-one" conveys such a meaning as combining the heaven, the earth and the human beings into one so as to be immortal. In short, no matter what the explanation is like, the three-in-one posture is not only the reflection of the concordance of internal and external, but also an excellent exercise for comprehensive training.

The three-in-one posture sets strict demands on every part of the body. Beginners should practise assiduously and constantly to grasp the essentials so that a solid foundation can be established for enhancing the technical level of Xingyiquan.

1) The Stance (the legs)

The Three-in-one posture

To form a three-in-one posture, you should stand with one foot in front. Place the other foot in a straight line directly behind the front heel, toes pointing obliquely outward. Bend both knees but keep your weight mainly on the rear leg. The rear foot should press backward and the front foot should push forward against the ground with the toes grasping the ground tightly so as to prop the body up firmly. You should keep the toes of your front foot, the tip of your nose and the tip of the forefinger of the hand that is stretched out in a same vertical plane. Yet you can assume the three-in-one posture in three different ways.

To put on a three-in-one posture in a high stance, you are required to stand with the rear foot about one and a half foot-lengths behind the front heel. Bend the rear knee to an angle of about 150 degrees with the buttocks in a straight line directly above the rear heel. Distribute twenty percent of your weight onto the front leg and keep the rest on the rear one. This kind of stance is called the two-to-eight stance (Fig. 1-2). You can move quite agilely with this stance because of the relatively high centre of gravity and the small stride. However, such a stance is less firm and can not withstand a heavy bump.

If you are to take a three-in-one posture in a median stance, you must lengthen the distance between your feet to about two and half foot-lengths and further bend the rear knee to an angle of 140 degrees. You must assign thirty percent of your weight onto the front leg and maintain the rest on the rear one. This kind of stance is usually called the three-to-seven stance (Fig. 3). Practising with this one can help you increase your breathing capacity through expanding the chest. Because the three-in-one posture in a median stance is such as having the stride neight too big nor too small and being neither buoyant nor sluggish,

it is a good exercise for ordinary practitioners.

The three-in-one posture in a low stance is also called a "big frame." To assume such a posture, you should place your rear foot approximately four foot-lengths behind the front heel and bend the rear knee to an angle of about 120 degrees, with fourty percent of your weight on the front leg and the other sixty percent on the rear one, thus forming a four-to-six stance (Fig. 4). As the stride is big and the centre of gravity is low, this stance functions well in building up your strength, especially that of your lower limbs.

2) The Head

The head is the commander of the whole body. Without an upright head, there are no perfect body position and balance. You should straighten your neck so as to hold your head well up. Do not tilt your head to any side. Concentrate your attention and look horizontally forward. You should draw your chin slightly in and close your mouth naturally with the tongue gently pressing upward. Be sure to maintain a natural but earnest facial expression.

3) The Torso

While assuming the three-in-one posture, you have to draw your chest naturally in. Neither should you thrust your chest out, nor should you contract it excessively to such an extent as to be hunchbacked. As the saying goes: the chest appropriately drawn in enables the vital energy to drop; the chest thrust out causes the vital energy to surge high; the lifted chest forces the vital energy to get together; whereas the sunken chest restrains the vital energy.

The abdomen should be solidified. Do not protrude the belly or draw it inward deliberately. You have to guide your vital energy down to "dantian" with abdominal respiration so as to make the belly more tenacious and resilient. Moreover, you are required to keep your back extended, waist dropped and buttocks tucked in, thus shaping them into a smooth segment of an arc.

To sum up, you should maintain an upright torso and turn it about 45 degrees to the side. Be sure not to bend forward or lean backward.

4) The Shoulders and Arms

Keep your shoulders relaxed and do not shrug them at any time so that the energy stream and blood can flow smoothly to the arms. See that both your shoulders push forth slightly and naturally. Only in this way can you perfectly draw your chest in, extend the muscles on your back, impels the vital energy to go down and accumulate your strength.

To form a three-in-one posture, you should stretch your left arm forward with the elbow dropped and slightly bent. Hold your left hand with the wrist dropped, the palm cupped and facing the lower-front. Keep the five fingers separated from each other with the forefinger pointing upward. Expand the thumb extremely away from forefinger so that the two take the shape of half a circle. Bend your right elbow, keeping the arm well rounded, the wrist dropped, and place the root of the thumb close against the abdomen with the hollow of the hand facing downward.

5) The Breathing

You should apply abdominal respiration to breathe naturally, and manage to make your breathing deep, slow, smooth and even.

4. Four Tips

A tip is an end of something. But in Xingyiquan, the four tips refer to the hair, the tongue, the teeth and the fingers and toes.

1) The Hair

The ancients held that the hair, both on the head and on the body, was the tip of the blood or the gateway of the skin, reflecting the circulation of vital energy. Your hair bristles when you are in great excitement and full of vigilance. That means you should close your pores and strain your muscles as if shutting the gateway, so as to accumulate vital energy and increase inner power.

2) The Tongue

In the ancients' opinion, the tongue was the tip of flesh. Actually, some requirements have especially been set for the movements of the tongue while practising Xingyiquan. When you are performing ordinary movements, the tip of your tongue should touch the palate gently; while you are exerting strength, the tongue should push up tightly so as to promote force. On the other hand, the up-and-down movements of the tongue impels the salivary gland to secrete more saliva which can not only relieve you of an unbearable thirst in the exercise, but also bring about a good digestion.

3) The Teeth

The ancients believed that the teeth were the tip of bones. As the saying goes: "The power stored in bones can be effectively emitted only with the teeth clenched tight." So, at the moment you are putting forth your strength explosively, you should clench your teeth with great force as if you are about to bite an iron bar in two. You ought to increase your strength and promote the exertion of strength in this manner.

4) The Fingers and The Toes

The fingers and the toes are the ends of our limbs, and they are often called the tip of tendons which play an important role in every movement of the body. Particularly, the strength of your hands depends to a large extent on the thickness and tenacity of the tendons on your hands. An ancient boxing manual said: "Claws are the vanguards of mighty tigers and fiece eagles." It can work wonders in actual combat to make a grab with hands and stamp with feet. So, martial artists of the ages always deemed highly of the finger exercises. And you should take them seriously in order to enhance elasticity and tenacity of the tendons on the hands as well as to fortify the metacarpals and the phalanges.

5. Four Images

In Xingyiquan, the four images refer to the cock, the dragon, the bear and the tiger. The cock exercise takes the skillfulness of a cock standing on one leg; the dragon exercise reflects the miraculous nimbleness of a dragon with a flexible body; the bear exercise embodies the martial prowess of a bear with powerful shoulders; and the tiger exercise incarnates the fierce expression of a tiger springing on its prey.

1) The Cock's Leg

A cock can run nimbly with big strides. It can also stop all of a sudden into a one-leg standing but balance itself very well. What is called "the cock's leg" in Xingyiquan is just such a posture as standing on one leg with the other lifted, and it actually means to place your weight largely on one leg and keep the other empty. Inevitably you are sluggish if you put your weight evenly on both legs; but it is true that you can move skillfully with only one leg to bear much of the weight. The essential of "the cock's leg" is to shift weight precisely between the legs so that you can advance,

retreat, rise, fall, turn round or change forms freely, nimbly and quickly.

2) The Dragon's Body

A dragon is an imaginary animal in ancient Chinese fables. It is said that a dragon is capable of expanding, contracting, mounting the clouds and riding the mist. The reason why Xingyiquan sets a high value upon "the dragon's body" is that every transitional movement of Xingyiquan should embody the feature of a dragon's body. For instance, when you huddle yourself up to accumulate strength, you should be like a dormant dragon waiting for a chance to show its prowess; and when you rouse to launch an attack, you should act like a rising dragon exhibiting towering majesty.

3) The Bear's Shoulders

Bears are huge animals endowed with extraordinary power, especially in their shoulders. As we have stated before, shoulders are the base sections of the upper limbs, determining the expanding force of the arms to a great extent. Xingyiquan thinks highly of the bear's shoulders on purpose to call practitioners' attention to storing up strength in the shoulders. If your shoulders are slack, the force of the hands, forearms and elbows would be like water without a source, or a tree without roots.

4) The Tiger's head

Tigers are the most ferocious animals of the world and they are considered as the kind of all animals. The boldness, decisiveness and marvelous quickness manifested by a tiger springing on its prey are really astonishing, and they are the characteristics needed for practising Xingyiquan. This is the reason why Xingyiquan specially mentions "the tiger's head." Generally speaking, you should always express great majesty through your head, exhibit imposing manner on your face, show prowess through your eyes, store up strength in your body, prepare your limbs for launching an attack at any time and assume an ambush posture just as a tiger does.

6. Five Elements

Xingyiquan was created in the light of the ancient Chinese theories of the five elements. The five elements, metal, wood, water, fire and earth, expound the mutual promotion and restraint of natural phenomena. The principles were particularly applied to attack-defence technique and health-building, thereby came the five-element boxing consisting of chop palm, punch fist, drill fist, cannon fist and

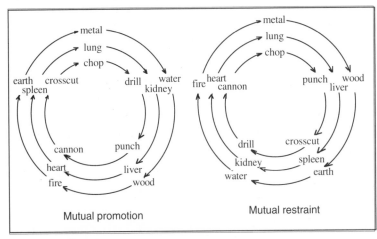

Mutual promotion

Mutual restraint

crosscut fist.

The mutual promotion and restraint of the five elements and correspondingly the five boxing methods are as follows: metal gives birth to water, water to wood, wood to fire, fire to earth and earth to metal; whereas metal restrains wood, wood restrains earth, earth restrains water, water restrains fire and fire restrains metal. Likewise, chop leads to drill, drill to punch, punch to cannon, cannon to crosscut and crosscut to chop; but chop suppresses punch, punch suppresses crosscut, crosscut suppresses drill, drill suppresses cannon and cannon suppresses chop.

7. Six Conformities

In Xingyiquan, the six conformities refer to the three internal and the three external ones. The three internal conformities include those of mind and will, will and vital energy, vital energy and strength. Just as an ancient statement goes: "The mind is the marshal, the will is the order, the vital energy is the vanguard and the strength is the soldier." The three external conformities consist of those of hands and feet, elbows and knees, shoulders and hips.

The conformity of mind and will means that if you have a mind to do something, you should have the same will. That is to say, the will must follow the mind in order to reach perfect harmony of the movements. The conformity of will and vital energy indicates that the will must guide the vital energy. Wherever the will goes, the vital energy should flow in the same direction. The conformity of vital energy and strength concerns the way to exert strength. You are required to use you vital energy to promote your strength so that you can exert the inner power explosively to hit your opponent and cause him to fall.

To achieve the conformity of hands and feet, you should first harmonize your movements in appearance with the hands and the feet reaching the definite position at the same time. You should then strive to apply integrated strength, keeping the initiative in your own hands to take the offensive or defensive. Moreover, you are required to coordinate both your arms as well as both your legs. The thrust of one hand should be in good concordance with the withdrawal of the other. Both the forearms should move against the flanks in opposite directions. When you take a step forward, the rear foot should go brushing along the inner side of the front foot. With the upper and the lower body well combined into one, the integrated strength is no longer the inaccessible.

The conformity of elbows and knees suggests that you should first of all harmonize both your elbows, so that you would not fall into such an awkward position as having a feeble middle section thus making your move loose effectiveness. Next, you should harmonize both your knees so as to strengthen your lower limbs and stabilize your stance. It also concerns the concordance of the elbow with the knee on the other side as well as the knee on the same side. You have to bring your elbows and knees into line so that you can carry out every move freely, nimbly, smoothly and steadily.

Shoulders and hips are the base sections of the limbs. In practising Xingyiquan, you should manage to achieve the conformity of these big joints. Good coordination of the shoulder with the hip of the opposite side as well as the hip of the same side binds the bases closely together, stabilizing you like Mount Taishan. For instance, when you do "the chop palm in forward step", the right foot should go forward and step on the ground with great force originated from the hip which turns in the same direction. Meanwhile, the right shoulder should push forth so as to cooperate

with the right hip. While with "the punch fist in forward step", when the left foot goes ahead and the right fist thrusts forward, you should twist your waist, drawing the left shoulder back and pushing the right shoulder forth.

To sum up, Xingyiquan requires you to combine the internal and the external into one, to harmonize the upper and the lower body, and to bring the left and the right sides into line, so that the whole body can be turned into a highly-unified entity.

8. Basic Rules and Methods

1) Body Form (The Motionless Position)

Stand upright with your legs together, tiptoes pointing obliquely outward, shoulders relaxed and lowered, arms hanging down, chest naturally drawn in. Do not throw your belly out or protrude your buttocks. Keep your neck erect and head well up with the chin slightly pulled in as if carrying a pitcher on your head. Look horizontally forward. (Fig. 5-6)

2) Hand Pattern

a) The Arched Palm:
Cup the palm into a shallow scoop with the four fingers naturally separated from each other and the thumb extremely apart from the up-pointing forefinger (Fig. 7-8). This common used palm is also called the "tiger's paw." You can apply this palm to strike forward, chop down, push up or sweep to and fro freely.

b) The Fist:
Close the four fingers and roll them into the hollow of the hand. Bend the thumb and place its first section over the second sections of the forefinger and the middle finger. Hold the fist tight and keep the forefist in a spiral. You form an upward fist when you turn the

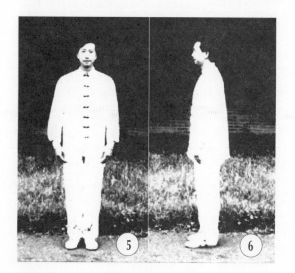

2

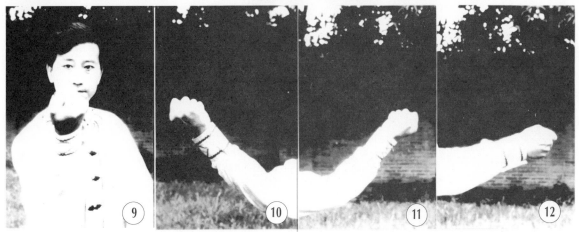

centre of the fist up (Fig. 9-11). If the eye of the fist is on top, it is a standing fist (Fig. 12). Fists are most frequently used in Xingyiquan.

3) Stances

c) The Hook:

Bend the hand at the wrist with the little finger, the ring finger, the middle finger and the forefinger successively folding down, and place the first section of the thumb upon those of the forefinger and the middle finger. (Fig. 13)

a) Three-in-one Stance:

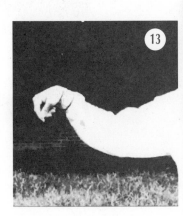

Stand upright with one foot in front, the knee slightly beat and the toes pointing forward. Place the rear foot about 20 to 60 cm directly behind the front heel with the toes pointing about 45 degrees to the side. Bend the rear knee to drop

17

to a semi-squat. (Fig. 14)

b) T-stance:
Bend one leg to drop to a semi-squat. Bend the other leg and place the tiptoes gently on the ground next to the weight-bearing foot. (Fig. 15)

c) Horse-riding Stance:

Stand upright with the feet to the sides and about three foot-lengths apart from each other, the toes pointing forward. Bend both knees to drop to a semi-squat with both thighs almost level. (Fig. 16)

d) Semi-horse-riding Stance:

Stand upright with one leg in front, the knee bent and the toes turned a little inward. Place the rear foot about three foot-lengths behind

front one with the toes pointing outward. Bend the rear leg to drop to a semi-squat, keeping your weight mainly on the rear leg. (Fig. 17)

e) Crouch Stance:

Bend one leg at the knee completely and drop to a full squat with the buttock close to the heel, the toes pointing obliquely outward. Stretch the other leg sideways with the knee straightened and the toes turned inward. Set both soles flat on the ground. (Fig. 18)

f) Empty Stance:
Stand with one leg in front. Bend the rear leg at the knee and drop to a semi-squat with the toes pointing about 45 degrees outward. Keep your weight on the rear leg. Bend the front leg at the knee with the toes resting gently on the ground. (Fig. 19-20)

g) Bow Stance:
Stand with one foot in front and the other a stride behind. Bend the front leg at the knee

until the thigh is almost level and the knee in a straight line above the toes. Straighten the rear leg with the heel pressing backward, the toes pointing about 45 degrees outward. (Fig. 21)

h) One-leg Stance (Cock Stance):

Stand on one leg and bend the knee slightly to take a high squat. Raise the other leg and

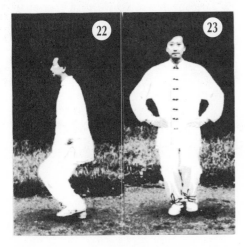

place the foot next to the ankle of the weight-bearing leg. (Fig. 22-23)

i) Seated Stance:

Cross legs with one in front and the other at the back. Bend both legs to drop to a full squat, keeping the whole sole of the front foot on the ground with the toes pointing outward, and resting your buttocks on the calf of the rear leg with the heel raised. (Fig. 24)

4) Footwork

a) Forward Step:

The rear foot takes a step forward, or the front foot goes half a step forward.

b) Backward Step:

The front foot takes a step backward.

c) Follow-up Step:

Immediately after the front foot moves forward, the rear foot follows up with half a step and again lands behind the front one.

d) Retreat Step:

Immediately after the rear foot moves backward, the front foot backs with half a step and again lands in front of the rear one.

e) Change Step:

The front foot and the rear foot change their position.

f) Ankle-brushing Step (Example of the left three-in-one stance):

The left foot takes half a step forward. The right foot immediately comes up, pausing just for a short time beside the ankle of the left leg, then continues to advance swiftly. As soon as the right foot lands, the left foot comes up, pausing just for a short time beside the ankle of the right leg, then continues to advance swiftly. Once the left foot lands in front, the right foot follows up with half a step, forming a left three-in-one stance again. (Fig. 25-35)

quickly and pause for a moment, then go forward brushing past the inner side of the ankle of the weight-bearing leg.

g) Turn Step (Example of the right three-in-one stance):

2

The front foot should move as far ahead as possible. The rear foot should comes up

The body turns round to the left with the toes of the right foot swung inward and those of the left foot outward. You thus form a left

three-in-one stance. (Fig. 36-38)

h) Hopping Step (Example with the right foot in front):

The left foot moves forward, with a big step and pushes off the ground to jump up. Swing the right leg upward with the knee bent at the same time. As soon as the left foot lands, the right foot goes to the front. (Fig. 39-50)

The step should be carried out swiftly and powerfully so as to bring the body high into the air. The landing must be firm.

Chapter Three

Five-element Boxing

The Five-element Boxing is composed of the most fundamental methods of Xingyiquan, i. e. chop palm, drill fist, punch fist, cannon fist and crosscut fist. It was so named because the methods were held as the representatives of the five elements, metal, wood, water, fire and earth, which, the ancients believed, constituted the physical universe.

The movements of the Five-element Boxing are simple, uncomplicated and un-adorned but regular and compact. You can practise a left form then a right form alternately. Owing to the differences in strength application among various methods, beginners should exercise conscientiously so as to lay a solid foundation.

According to the theory of mutual promotion and restraint of the five elements, the appropriate sequence of practice is usually so set: first, the chop palm; then the drill fist; then the punch fist; afterwards the cannon fist and finally the crosscut fist.

1. Chop Palm

The chop palm, representing metal, occupies the first place of the five methods. The movements look like chopping with an axe. The edge of an axe is for cutting and the back of an axe is for smashing. Correspondingly, there are two ways of practice. One is with the palm and the other is with the fist, the former meaning the use of the edge of an axe and the latter standing for the use of the back of an axe. Although the two differ in appearance and meaning, the principle is the same.

While practising Chop Palm, you should pay attention to your breathing. Inhale while you withdraw hands or huddle up, and exhale while you thrust hands or extend the body.

There are also two purposes in employing the chop palm. One is only to bent back the enemy, and the other is to chop, using the palm as a knife, at the enemy's face, neck, chest, ribs or belly in order to wound him. Usually the emphasis is placed on the latter.

Preparatory Form

(1)

Stand upright with your legs together, tiptoes pointing obliquely outward, arms hanging down naturally. Look horizontally forward.

(2-4)

Raise your arms slowly and respectively from the front-left and the front-right to shoulder level with hollows of the hands facing downward.

(5-9)

Bend both knees and drop to a semi-squat as you turn your torso slightly to the right. Clench both your fists in the meantime. The fists then get close in front of the face and slowly drop to the front of the abdomen with the forefists facing each other and the centres of the fists facing downward.

(10-11)

As you turn your torso slightly to the left, the right fist rises with the centre of the fist turned up, and then thrusts passing before the chin to the front, the elbow slightly bent and lowered, the forearm rotated outward, the forefist in a spiral and the little finger in a straight line just before the tip of the nose.

(12-14)

The left foot takes a big step forward. The right foot immediately follows up with half a step to form a left three-in-one stance, the weight mainly on the right leg. At the same time, with the centre of the fist turned up, the left fist rises, passing before the chest and chin, then changes into a palm and chops to the front at shoulder level with the elbow slightly bent and lowered, the hollow of the hand facing the lower-front, the force concentrated on the base of the palm; while the right fist changes into a palm and withdraws until the root of the thumb gets close against the abdomen with the hollow of the hand facing downward. You thus form a three-in-one

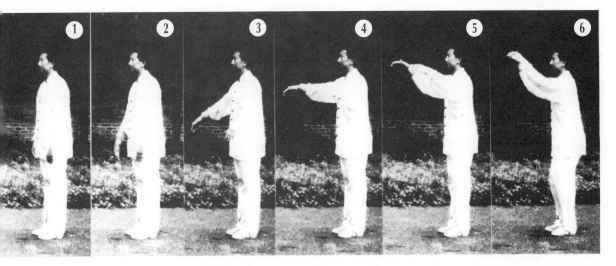

3

posture.

Points to remember:

You should set your eyes toward the front, keep your body upright, neck erect, teeth gently closed, and maintain a natural facial expression throughout the form. The chop of the left palm and the step of the left foot should be well harmonized. When the hands come up and move inward, you should inhale; and when you squat yourself down, you should exhale. Likewise, inhaling should accompany the thrust of the right fist, and exhaling should accompany the chop of the left palm.

25

Right Chop Palm in Forward Step

(15-16)

With the palm changing into a fist, the left hand goes downward and backward to the front of the abdomen. Clench the right fist and turn centres of both your fists up in the meantime, keeping both the forearms tightly against the flanks. Look straight ahead.

(17-19)

Propelled by a powerful drive of the right foot, the left foot takes half a step forward with the toes turned about 45 degrees outward. As you bend the left knee slightly and shift your weight

completely onto the left leg, bring the right foot next to the left ankle with the sole apart from the ground and the toes pointing forward. At the same time, the left fist rises, passing before the chest and the chin, then thrusts to the front at nose level, the elbow slightly bent and lowered.

(20-22)

The right foot takes a big step forward. The left foot immediately follows up with half a step to form a right three-in-one stance, the weight mainly on the left leg. At the same time, the right fist rises, passing before the chest and the chin, then changes into a palm and chops to the front at shoulder level with the elbow slightly bent and lowered, the hollow of the hand facing the lower-front, the force concentrated on the base of the palm; while the left fist changes into

a palm and withdraws until the root of the thumb gets close against the abdomen with the hollow of the hand facing downward. Look in the direction of the forefinger of the right hand.

Points to remember:

As you withdraw the left fist at the beginning of this form, you should maintain a firm stance and hold the arms close against your flanks as if exerting your utmost effort to pull nine bulls down. You should inhale and guide your energy stream down to "dantian (lower abdomen)" in the meantime. Then, you should finish the thrust of the left fist in cooperation with the advance of the left foot, and with great impulsive force. See that your shoul-

3

ders are level and you keep your balance through the one-leg position. Finally, you should conduct the chop of the right palm with the right foot taking a big but steady stride as if having the momentum with which to chop eight horses down.

Left Chop Palm in Forward Step

(23-29)

These are the reversed movements of the Right Chop Palm in Forward Step. Repeat them in the same manner as shown in Figures 15-22, only in the opposite direction, substituting "left" for "right" and vice versa.

Right Chop Palm in Forward Step

(30-34)

The same as those described in Figures 15-22.

Chop Palm Turn

(35-37)

Turn your torso to the left with the toes of the right foot turned in, and shift much of the weight onto the right leg. At the same time, clench both your fists. The right fist moves to the left, passing before the face, then drops until it gets close against the abdomen. Keep both arms appropriately bent with the forefists facing each other, the centres of the fists facing downward, and exert back-holding force through the elbows. Turn your head to look to the left just at the moment the right fist reaches the abdomen.

(38-40)

Turn your torso to the left and turn centres of both fists up. The left foot immediately takes a step forward with the toes turned out. As you bend the left knee slightly and shift your weight completely onto the left leg, bring the right foot next to the left ankle with the sole apart from the ground and the toes pointing forward. At the same time, the left fist rises, passing before the chest and the chin, then thrusts to the front at nose level, the elbow slightly bent and lowered. Look in the direction of the left fist.

(41-42)

The right foot takes a big step forward. The left foot immediately follows up with half a step

to form a right three-in-one stance, the weight mainly on the left leg. At the same time, the right fist rises, passing before the chest and the chin, then changes into a palm and chops to the front at shoulder level with the elbow slightly bent and lowered, the hollow of the hand facing the lower-front, the force concentrated on the base of the palm; while the left fist changes into a palm and withdraws until the root of the thumb gets close against the abdomen with the hollow of the hand facing downward. Look in the direction of the forefinger of the right hand.

2. Drill Fist

Of the five methods, the drill fist is re-garded as the representative of water which can wind continuously, leaving no opening to penetrate through. Just as people say:"Drill Fist is like lightning", for the movements are swift, nimble and fierce. Talking of hand methods, the drill fist is such as drilling forward with one fist and pressing downward with the other palm (or fist). Both hands take turns to drill or press. The forward drill is for an attack, yet the downward press is for interception of an assault. When the advance of one foot is accompanied by the thrust of the hand on the same side, it is a smooth-step drill; if the front foot is the one on the opposite side to the thrusting fist, it is a twisted-step drill. However, the smooth-step drill is practised more often. As you conduct the drill fist, you are required to step and strike abruptly and vigorously, exerting explosive strength when you get near your opponent. You should practise arduously so as to be able to perform with the body as nimble as a monkey and the hands as flexible as a snake.

Furthermore, you should focus twisting force on the foremost end of the fist as if boring through whatever you meet.

There are three ways of applying drill fist: up-drill, horizontal-drill and down-drill. The up-drill aims at the opponent's face, eyes, temples and throat, the horizontal-drill at the opponent's chest and the down-drill at the opponent's belly.

Preparatory Form

(43)

Assume the left three-in-one posture as described in Chapter Two.

Right Drill Fist in Forward Step

(44-46)

The left foot takes half a step forward with the toes turned about 45 degrees out. As you shift your weight completely onto the left leg,

bring the right foot next to the left ankle with the sole apart from the ground and the toes pointing forward. At the same time, with the arm rotating inward and the elbow further bent, the left palm presses to the right and downward in front of the chest; while the right palm changes into a fist and begins to rise with the centre of the fist turned up.

(47-48)

The right foot takes a big step forward. The left foot immediately follows up with half a step to form a right three-in-one stance, the weight mainly on the left leg. At the same time, the left palm changes into a fist and withdraws until it gets close against the abdomen with the centre of the fist facing downward. Meanwhile, the right fist continues to rise, passing before the chest

and the chin, then drills from above the left fist to the front at mouth level with the elbow slightly bent and lowered. Keep the tip of your nose, the foremost end of the right fist and the tiptoes of the right foot in a same vertical plane when you finish the form. Look straight ahead.

Points to remember:

The press of the left palm and the advance of the left foot must synchronize perfectly. You should apply wrapping strength to the press. The right foot should move forward only after a short pause beside the left ankle, but not stop for long. You have to twist your torso to the left be-

fore you thrust the right fist forward for the purpose to accumulate strength. Finally, you should coordinate the forward step of the right foot and the drilling of the right fist so as to exert your utmost power in a flash.

Left Drill Fist in Forward Step

(49-51)

The right foot takes half a step forward with the toes turned about 45 degrees out. As you shift your weight completely onto the right leg, bring the left foot next to the right ankle with the sole apart from the ground and the toes pointing forward. At the same time, with the arm rotating inward and the elbow further bent, the right fist changes into a palm and presses to the left and

31

downward in front of the chest; while the left fist begins to rise with the centre of the fist turned up.

(52-54)

The left foot takes a big step forward. The right foot immediately follows up with half a step to form a left three-in-one stance, the weight mainly on the right leg. At the same time, the right palm changes into a fist and withdraws until it gets close against the abdomen with the centre of the fist facing downward. Meanwhile, the left fist continues to rise, passing before the chest and the chin, then drills from above the right fist to the front at mouth level with the elbow slightly bent and lowered. Look straight ahead.

Drill Fist Turn

(55-56)

Turn your torso about 180 degrees to the right with the toes of the left foot turned in and those of the right foot out. Along with the turn of the body, the left fist sweeps horizontally round.

(57-59)

The right foot takes half a step forward. The left foot immediately follows up with half a step to form a right three-in-one stance, the weight mainly on the left leg. At the same time, with the arm rotating inward to turn the centre of the fist down, the left fist presses downward until it gets

close against the abdomen. Simultaneously, the right fist rises, passing before the chest and the chin, then drills from above the left fist to the front at mouth level, the centre of the fist facing upward. Look straight ahead.

Points to remember:

As you swing the left arm round, you should exert strength from the waist and the shoulder without any slackness. After the turn, you should carry out the step and the drilling immediately with great impulsive force. When you finish with the above movements, you can either repeat the left and the right forms of the drill fist in turn, or proceed to the punch fist.

3. Punch Fist

Punch fist, notable for its promptness and sharpness, represents wood of the five elements. As wood can turn to arrows, so goes the ancient statement: "Punch fist is like an arrow." As a matter of fact, the punch fist is practised more often in half a step. You always place the left foot in front and move it half a step forward when you carry out the punch. Therefore, if you thrust your left fist out, it is a smooth-step punch; whereas if you strike with your right fist, it is a twisted-step punch. The two fists take turns thrusting forward.

While practising the punch fist, you should have regard for the following aspects: The whole body must be imbued with irresistible force that is originated from the rear foot driving backward, transmitted to the hips and waist, conducted to the shoulders and elbows, and finally brought to the ends of the fists. See that you hold the arm close to the body, and apply spiral strength through your hips, waist, shoulder and arm so as to thrust the fist out like a drill, with the elbow brushing against the flank of the body. The withdrawal of the fist must be finished in the same manner and with an overturn at first. All the movements, including those of the torso, legs, arms and the breathing, must be carried out smoothly. Speaking particularly, you should have the will and momentum of thrusting your fist like an arrow shot from a bow so as to pierce through your enemy's body with the suddenness of a thunderbolt while he is unprepared.

In short, punch fist can produce tremendous impulsive force and cause intense shock, thus giving the enemy a heavy blow. You can strike the enemy at the face with an up-punch, or directly at the chest with a horizontal-punch, or at the upper abdomen with a down-punch.

Preparatory Form

(60)

Assume the left three-in-one posture as de-scribed in Chapter Two.

Right Punch Fist in Forward Step

3

(61)

Clench both your fists tight in spirals. Turn the centre of the right fist up, and move the left fist a little down with the elbow slightly bent, the forearm at chest level and the eye of the fist on top.

(62-64)

Propelled by a powerful drive of the right foot, the left foot takes as big as possible a step forward. The right foot immediately follows up with half a step to form a left three-in-one stance, the weight mainly on the right leg. At the same time, the left fist withdraws to the left side of the waist with the centre of the fist facing upward; while the right fist punches straight ahead like an arrow, with the torso twisted to the left, the right shoulder pushed forth, the elbow slightly bent and the eye of the fist on top. Concentrate the force on the foremost end of the right fist. Look in the direction of the right fist.

Points to remember:

Inhale and twist your torso slightly to the left in advance so as to accumulate strength before the steps begin. You should act smoothly and steadily, neither lifting the body nor raising the feet too far off the ground. As you thrust the

right fist forward, you must exhale to promote strength.

Left Punch Fist in Forward Step

(65-67)

With the right foot forcibly driving the ground backward, ethe left foot advances as far as possible. The right foot immediately follows up with half a step to form a left three-in-one stance, the weight mainly on the right leg. At the same time, the right fist withdraws to the right side of the waist with the centre of the fist facing upward; while the left fist punches straight ahead, the elbow slightly bent and the eye of the fist on top. Look in the direction of the fist. Now you can repeat the right and the left forms of the punch fist in turn.

Punch Fist Turn

(68-70)

Turn your torso round to the right with the toes of the left foot turned in. Then, shift your weight onto the left leg and raise the right leg with the up-bumping force, the knee bent, the foot hooked and the toes turned out. Simultaneously, the left fist moves in an arc to the right with the elbow bent, and then drops to the front of the abdomen with the centre of the fist facing downward; while the right fist rises, passing before the chest and the chin, then drills to the front,

the elbow slightly bent, the centre of the fist facing upward.

(71-73)

As the right foot lands to the front with the toes still turned out, bent both knees to squat yourself down with the legs tightly crossed, thus forming a seated stance. At the same time, the right fist changes into a palm and pulls downward and backward until it pauses behind the right hip, the elbow slightly bent; while the left fist rises, passing before the chest and the chin, then changes into a palm and chops to the lower-front, the elbow slightly bent, the hollow of the hand facing the lower-front. Look in the direction of the left hand.

Points to remember:

The turn of the body, the lift of the leg and the drill of the fist must be linked up smoothly and continuously. The chop of the left palm must coincide with the landing of the right foot. Be sure not to hang your head or bend the torso when you squat down to form the seated stance. After the turn, you can go on practising with the above movements. The transitional way is as follows: Stand a little up with the right foot moving half a step forward. The left foot then takes a step forward to form a left three-in-one stance. At the same time, the left palm changes into a fist and withdraws to the left side of the waist with the centre of the fist facing upward; while the right

hand changes into a fist and punches to the front with the eye of the fist on top.

4. Cannon Fist

As the symbolization of fire, the cannon fist is imbued with great explosive power. It reflects the conformity of will, vital energy and strength with the apparent opening and closing of the body movements. When you conduct closing movements, you should hold back will, collect vital energy and accumulate strength; whereas when you carry out opening movements, you should act under the guide of the will, breathe out and exert strength.

The way to apply strength in practising cannon fist can be brought under four words: Wrapping, pulling, rolling and bursting. Wrapping strength refers to the inward or embracing force which makes you seemingly soft but indeed powerful. Pulling strength concerns the downward and backward force which is applied to the withdrawal of the hands. Rolling strength means that you should twist your torso and rotate your arms appropriately. For instance, when you perform the "uphold fist". you should rotate the arm inward through the process; when you advance and punch forward, you should twist the torso and thrust the fist like a drill bit. Bursting strength depicts the ordinary way of strength exertion, meaning that you should concentrate force on the particular striking point accurately, thus, with the movement picking up speed, there appears at the end of the move a sudden snap-strike like an explosion of a shell. Cannon Fist, as well as Punch Fist and Drill Fist, has great impulsive force, and is therefore powerful in an offensive. But its outstanding virtue lies on the method of launching an attack while acting on the defensive. Usually you take a step obliquely forward to form a twisted stance, hold one fist up to ward off a blow from your opponent,and thrust the other fist directly at your opponent's vital part such as the face, throat or chest.

3

Preparatory Form

(74)

Assume the left three-in-one posture as described in Chapter Two.

Left Cannon Fist in Forward Step

(75-77)

As you turn your torso slightly to the left, the left foot takes a step to the front-left. Shift your weight onto the left leg and bring the right foot next to the left ankle with the sole apart from the ground. At the same time, both hands first stretch to the upper-front, and then grasp downward until

they get to the sides of the abdomen with centres of the fists turned up.

(78-79)

As you turn your torso slightly to the right, the right foot takes a big step to the front-right. The left foot immediately follows up with half a step to form a right three-in-one stance. At the

same time, the right fist drills upward, passing before the chest and the face, then, with the forearm rotating inward, pushes to the front of the right part of the forehead, the arm raised and rounded, the centre of the fist facing the front. Simultaneously, the left fist thrusts to the front-right at chest level with the elbow slightly bent and the eye of the fist on top. Look in the direc-

36

tion of the left fist.

Points to remember:

The pull of the hands must coincide with the advance of the left foot. You should apply wrapping strength as if binding up a firecracker which can go off with greater power when wrapped up tight. Before the right foot steps to the front-right, you ought to turn your torso to the right in advance so as to accumulate strength. You should coordinate the upholding of the right arm and the thrust of the left fist too.

Right Cannon Fist in Forward Step

(80-82)

The right foot takes a step to the front-right. As you shift your weight onto the right leg, bring the left foot next to the right ankle with the sole apart from the ground. At the same time, both hands first change into palms and stretch to the upper-front, and then grasp downward and backward until they get to the sides of the abdomen with centres of the fists turned up.

(83-85)

As you turn your torso slightly to the left, the left foot takes a big step to the front-left. The right foot immediately follows up with half a step to form a left three-in-one stance. At the same time, the left fist drills upward passing before

the chest and the face, then, with the forearm rotating inward, pushes to the front of the left part of the forehead, the arm raised and rounded, the centre of the fist facing the front. Simultaneously, the right fist thrusts to the front-left at chest level with the elbow slightly bent and the eye of the fist on top. Look in the direction of the right fist.

Cannon Fist Turn

(86)

Turn your torso round to the right with the toes of the left foot turned in and those of the right foot out. Both the arms sweep round along with the turn of the body .

(87-93)

The same as those described in Figures 80-85, only in the opposite direction, substituting "left" for "right" and vice versa.

Points to remember:

You should turn round swiftly and smoothly, then proceed to the left cannon fist, leaving no pause in between. When you finish with the above movements, you can repeat the right and the left forms of the cannon fist alternately, the number of repetition depending upon the space and your bodily power.

5. Crosscut Fist

The crosscut fist represents earth which, according to the principles of the five elements, is the mother of all things. Likewise, crosscut is regarded as the base on which grow the chop palm, the drill fist, the punch fist and the cannon fist. So there goes a saying, "Always make opening moves with crosscut fists."

When you practise with the crosscut fist, you should put stress on the development of "rolling strength" and "springing strength."

You must advance or retreat with the torso twisted. When you thrusts a fist out, the hand must crosscut and rotate as it goes along. The moment the fist is about to reach the target, the legs, waist, shoulders and arms should act harmoniously, exerting strong power which makes the fist shake and spring vigorously.

Crosscut Fist is such a skill as striking a blow while fending off an attack. For instance, if the opponent pushes on, you can first crosscut his arm with your fist, and then continues to thrust the fist forward to strike the opponent directly at the chest or at the throat.

Preparatory Form

(94)

Assume the left three-in-one posture as described in Chapter Two.

Right Crosscut Fist

(95)

Turn your torso slightly to the left and clench both your fists. The right fist rises to the front of the chest and then, with the forearm twisting outward forcibly, thrusts from beneath the left forearm to the front at mouth level, the elbow slightly bent, the centre of the fist turned up. Simultaneously, the left fist moves backward and presses downward, pausing just under the right elbow with the centre of the fist facing downward. Look at the right fist.

Points to remember:

You should carry out this form with the two arms acting in opposite directions as if twisting a towel. The right fist must imbued with great transverse rolling force as well as great forward momentum.

Left Crosscut Fist in Forward Step

(96-100)

The left foot takes half a step to the front-left. Without any pause, the right foot goes along, passing beside the left foot and moves with a big step to the front-right. The left foot immediately follows up with half a step to form a right three-in-one stance. At the same time, with the forearm twisting outward forcibly, the left fist thrusts from beneath the right forearm to the front at mouth level, the elbow slightly bent, the centre of the fist turned up. Simultaneously, the right fist moves backward and presses downward, pausing just before the abdomen with the centre of the fist turned down. Look at the left fist.

Points to remember:

The right foot must move with a giant stride along a curve. Be sure not to raise yourself during the step but be steady and even. You must combine the twisting strength of the torso and the arms with the impulsive force engendered by the drive of the legs to produce great integrated power.

Right Crosscut Fist in Forward Step

(101-106)

The same as those described in Figures 96-100, only in the opposite direction, substituting

"left" for "right" and vice versa.

40

Crosscut Fist Turn

(107-108)

Turn your torso round to the right with the toes of the left foot turned in and those of the right foot out. The right arm sweeps round along with the turn of the body .

(109-112)

The same as those described in Figures 96-100, except that the left foot takes a step to the front-left to begin with the rest movements.

3

6. Use of the Boxing Methods

1) The Use of Chop Palm

If the opponent thrusts his fist into your abdomen, you can press his wrist down with your hand of the same side, and simultaneously chop at his face or chest with your other palm (Fig. 113-118).

The timing must be opportune. You have to finish the press and the chop just before the opponent's fist reaches your body. Moreover, you must coordinate the whole body so as to carry out the chop swiftly and with great forward and downward force.

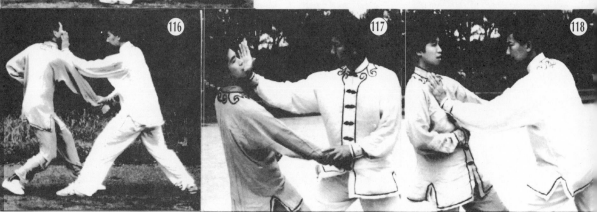

2) The Use of Drill Fist

If the opponent thrusts his right fist straight into your chest, you can press the oncoming fist down with your left hand, and simultaneously step forward with your right foot and drill into his throat or chest with your right fist (Fig. 119-123).

You must press the opponent's fist swiftly and accurately, and step forward to approach the opponent without the least hesitation. You must combine the spring force of the arm with the impulsive force produced by the forward step so as to carry out the drill fist powerfully.

3) The Use of Punch Fist

a) To launch an active attack, you can approach your opponent swiftly with a forward step of the left foot and a powerful drive of the right foot, and pluck aside the opponent's hand with your left hand and punch him straight into the belly with your right fist (Fig. 124-127).

b) If the opponent thrusts his fist at your face, you can pluck the oncoming fist with your left fist and hit back with your right fist (Fig. 128-129).

Punch fist must be carried out like an arrow shot out from a bow at full speed and with great piercing force.

c) The use of Punch Fist Turn: If the opponent thrusts his fist at your face, you can ward off the oncoming blow with your right fist and raise your right foot to tread on his knee (Fig. 130). You can also grab and twist the opponent's wrist with your right hand and chop him at the face with your left palm while you raise your right foot to tread on his knee (Fig. 131). You can kick the opponent either on the knee or on the belly. If you get close enough to the opponent, you can also raise your right knee to dash against his crotch.

4) The Use of Cannon Fist

If the opponent swoops forth with his right palm chopping at your face, you can meet him head-on, raising your left fist to ward off the oncoming blow and thrusting your right fist straight into his chest (Fig. 132-135).

When the opponent approaches, you should meet the attack calmly. Do not retreat but press on, therefore the opponent is unable to bring the momentum of his fist into full play. If you can take advantage of the impulsive force of the opponent, your counter-blow is undoubtedly more powerful. The forward step, the up-hold of the left fist and the thrust of the right fist must be conducted swiftly and opportunely, or the counter-blow will lose its effectiveness.

5) The Use of Crosscut Fist

If the opponent launches an attack at your throat with a drill fist, you can twist your torso swiftly and carry out a right crosscut fist to ward off the blow. You can then continue to exert strength and thrust your right fist straight into the opponent's throat or face (Fig. 136-139).

After you invalidate the oncoming fist, you must exploit the opponent's blunder to hit back. There must not be a break in between.

3

Chapter Four

Twelve-animal Style Boxing

4

The Twelve-animal Style Boxing is a general name for the twelve kinds of boxing which take the various shapes of dragon, tiger, monkey, horse, snake, cock, swallow, sparrow hawk, alligator, tai, eagle and bear, and mimic the ways those animals act. For instance, the dragon exercise imitates the rise and fall of a dragon and displays its capability of catching; the tiger exercise manifests a tiger's vigilance when it comes out of its lair and its boldness when it pounces on its prey; the monkey exercise exhibits the liveliness, agility and deftness of a monkey. Each of the exercises conforms with both the appearance and the manner of an animal, and is an organic combination of external forms and boxing skills.

There are even more methods for the hands, the legs and the body and more skills of attack-defence in these exercises than in the Five-element Boxing. By making constant practice of the twelve-animal style boxing, you can further heighten your consciousness of attack and defence, develop your ability to combat, as well as build up your health and mould your temperament so as to prolong your life.

Each of the twelve exercises lays emphasis on different aspects and gets different effects due to its distinctive style. Therefore, you may choose whatever you like among them according to your actual situation. If time and your physical strength permit, you had better increase the number of repetition gradually so as to obtain better effects. Usually, you are required to return to the original place where you start off, then finish up with the closing form.

1. Dragon Exercise

A dragon is a fairy creature in tales. It is said that with invincible and unpredictable power, the dragon is capable of flying up to the heavens and diving deep into the sea. The twelve-animal style boxing begins from dragon exercise for the purpose to attach

importance to the rise and fall of the body, the bending and stretching of the arms and the alternation of the footwork. The benefit you can get to your waist and legs is too wonderful for words. Usually, you are required to perform to and fro along straight lines. All the movements should be carried out smoothly and nimbly. While jumping, you should push off the ground forcibly with your foot so as to rise as high up as possible. On dropping, you should squat down cross-legged. Your hands, shaped like the powerful paws of a dragon, should be wielded up and down with twisting and wrapping force. You should give equal consideration to both attack and defence.

You can perfect your vitality with dragon exercise. While you are practising, you should guide your energy stream down to "dantian", harmonize the upper and the lower halves of the body, and combine the internal and the external into one. You should act swiftly and vigorously, with hardness and softness promoting each other, and express your spirit through your bright eyes just like a miraculous dragon travelling through the space.

1) Opening Form

(1)

Stand upright with the head erect, mouth closed, the tip of the tongue pushing gently upward against the hard palate, arms hanging down naturally. Hold the heels together with the toes pointing obliquely outward. Never throw your chest out, nor hump your back. Concentrate your attention and breathe naturally. Look horizontally forward.

(2-3)

Raise both your arms sideward to shoulder level with hollows of the hands facing downward.

(4-7)

As you bend both knees to form a semi-squat, turn your torso slightly to the right with the feet

swinging on the heels about 45 degrees in the same direction. Meanwhile, clench both your fists and move them upward and inward. Both fists then drop from before the face to the front of the abdomen with the forefists facing each other and the centres of the fists facing downward. Look straight ahead.

(8-10)

As you turn your torso slightly to the left, the right fist rises with the centre of the fist turned up and the forearm close against the flank, then drills from before the chin to the front, the right shoulder pushing forth, the elbow slightly bent, the centre of the fist facing obliquely upward and the second joint of the little finger in a straight

4

line just before the tip of the nose. Keep both shoulders level and concentrate the force on the forefist.

(11-13)

The left foot takes a giant step forward. The right foot immediately follows up with half a step to form a left three-in-one stance. At the same

time, the left fist rises with the centre of the fist turned up, then changes into a palm and chops from before the chin to the front at shoulder level, the elbow slightly bent, the hollow of the hand facing the lower-front, and the force concentrated on the base of the palm; while the right fist changes into a palm and withdraws until the root of the thumb gets close against the abdomen with

the hollow of the hand facing downward. Look straight ahead.

Points to remember:

Perform the above movements slowly but steadily. The left foot must stride swiftly and then push forth against the ground without any slackness in the knee when it lands in front.

The chop of the left palm must be in perfect harmony with the forming of the stance.

2) Dragon Form - Left Rise and Left Fall

(14-15)

As you further bend the knees, the left hand

makes a grab and draws back to the front of the abdomen. Clench your right fist and breathe in to accumulate strength in the meantime.

(16-17)

As you jump as high as possible with the feet pushing off the ground powerfully, the left fist drills up, passing before the chest and the chin, to the upper-front of the head. The right fist then follows to the front of the face.

(18)

While you are still in the air, the left fist changes into a palm and goes down to the front of the abdomen. The right fist abruptly changes into a palm and stretches forward in the meantime.

(19-21)

On landing with both feet, place the right foot in front and bend both knees to the full extent. You thus squat down swiftly to form a right seated stance with the legs tightly crossed. At the same time, the left palm goes up again, then chops from before the chin to the lower-front, the elbow slightly bent, the wrist lowered and the thumb stretching outward; while the right palm drops and draws backward to the side of the right hip, the elbow bent, the hollow of the hand facing the rear. Look straight ahead.

Points to remember:

You should wield your arms smoothly along circular paths. The chop of the left palm and the pull of the right hand must synchronize perfectly.

3) Dragon Form - Left Rise and Right Fall

(22)

As you unbend the legs to rise, the left hand makes a grab and draws back to the front of the abdomen; while the right palm changes into a fist and moves to the right side of the waist.

(23)

As you jump as high as possible with the feet pushing off the ground powerfully, the left fist drills up, passing before the chest and the chin, to the upper-front of the head. The right fist then follows to the front of the face.

(24-26)

On landing with both feet, place the left foot in front and bend both knees to the full extent. You thus squat down swiftly to form a left seated stance with the legs tightly crossed. At the same time, open both your fists. The right palm abruptly stretches forward and then chops to the lower-front, the elbow slightly bent, the wrist lowered and the thumb stretching outward; while the left palm drops and draws backward to the side of the left hip, the elbow bent, the hollow of the hand facing the rear. Look straight ahead.

Points to remember:

The upward drills of the fists should be well coordinated with the rise of the body. Likewise, the downward presses of the palms should be in perfect harmony with the fall of the body.

4) Dragon Form - Right Rise and Left Fall

(27-28)

As you unbend the legs to rise, the right hand makes a grab and draws back to the front of the abdomen; while the left palm changes into a fist and moves to the left side of the waist.

53

(29)

As you jump as high as possible with the feet pushing off the ground powerfully, the right fist drills up, passing before the chest and the chin, to the upper-front of the head. The left fist then follows to the front of the chin.

(30-32)

On landing with both feet, place the right foot in front and bend both knees to the full extent. You thus squat down swiftly to form a right seated stance with the legs tightly crossed. At the same time, open both your fists. The left palm abruptly stretches forward and then chops to the

lower-front, the elbow slightly bent, the wrist lowered and the thumb stretching outward; while the right palm drops and draws backward to the side of the right hip, the elbow bent, the hollow of the hand facing the rear. Look straight ahead.

5) Hop and Chop with Both Palms

(33)

As you slightly unbend the legs to rise, shift your weight forward. At the same time, the left hand makes a grab and draws backward; while the right palm changes into a fist and moves to the right side of the waist.

(34-35)

The left foot takes a step forward. At the same time, the left fist drills up, passing before the chest and the chin, then stretches forward. The right fist immediately follows to the front of the chest.

(36)

As you hop forward with the left foot pushing off the ground powerfully, the right leg swings forward with the foot kicking forth. At the same time, the right fist stretches forward from above the left arm, changing into a palm abruptly when it passes by the left hand; while the left fist changes into a palm and goes downward, backward and then upward to the front of the chest.

(37-38)

After you get a landing with the left foot, place the right foot in front with the toes turned outward. As you turn your torso slightly to the right, bend both knees to form a semi-squat with the legs crossed and the heel of the left foot lifted. At the same time, the right palm chops down and then withdraws to the side of the right hip. Following the right hand, the left palm stretches forward and chops down to chest level, the wrist lowered and the hollow of the hand facing the lower-front. Look straight ahead.

Points to remember.

You should make a quick stride and then hop forward vigorously. You should finish the kick of the right leg while the body is still in the air. The successive chops of the palms should be well coordinated with the forming of the semi-squat.

6) Right Punch in Forward Step

(39-41)

The left foot takes a giant step forward. The right foot immediately follows up with half a step to form a left three-in-one stance. Meanwhile, clench both your fists. The right fist punches straight ahead, the elbow slightly bent, the eye of the fist on top. The left fist simultaneously withdraws to the left side of the waist, the centre of the fist facing upward. Look straight ahead.

Points to remember:

you should step forward swiftly and thrust the fist out with integrated strength.

7) Left Punch

(42-43)

The left foot takes a step forward. The right foot immediately follows up with half a step to form a left three-in-one stance. At the same time, the left fist punches straight ahead, the eye of the fist on top; while the right fist withdraws to

the right side of the waist, the centre of the fist facing upward.

Points to remember:

you should execute the punch swiftly and vigorously without any hesitation.

8) Turning Form

(44-45)

Turn your body round to the right with the toes of the left foot swung inward and your weight mainly on the left leg. At the same time, bend the left elbow and rotate the arm inward.

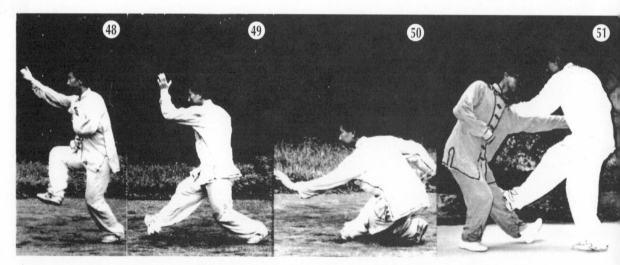

The left fist thus swings in an arc to the front of the abdomen. Both fists thus get close with the centres of the fists tightly against the belly.

(46-47)

Raise your right leg with the knee bent, the foot hooked and the toes turned outward. At the same time, the right fist rises, passing before the

chest and the chin, then drills to the front, the elbow slightly bent, the centre of the fist facing obliquely upward, and the second joint of the little finger in a straight line just before the tip of the nose.

(48-50)

As the right foot goes down in front, bend

both knees to form a right seated stance with the legs tightly crossed and the heel of the left foot lifted. At the same time, the left fist drills up, passing before the chest and the chin, then changes into a palm and chops to the lower-front, the elbow slightly bent and the wrist lowered. Simultaneously, the right fist changes into a palm and draws downward and backward to the side of the right hip, the elbow bent and the hollow of the hand facing the rear. Set your eyes toward the left palm.

Points to remember:

The turn of the body, as well as the movement of the left arm, should be carried out unhurriedly, resolutely and vigorously. The drill of the right fist and the rise of the right leg must synchronize perfectly. When you execute the chop in the seated stance, you should incline a little forward.

9) Dragon Form - Left Rise and Right Fall

The same as those described in Fig. 22-26, except that you are now performing the other way round.

10) Dragon Form - Right Rise and Left Fall

The same as those described in Fig. 27-32, except that you are now performing the other way round.

11) Hop and Chop with Both Palms

The same as those described in Fig. 33-38, except that you are now performing the other way round.

12) Right Punch in Forward Step

The same as those described in Fig. 39-41, except that you are now performing the other way round.

13) Left Punch

The same as those described in Fig. 42-43, except that you are now performing the other way round.

14) Turning Form

The same as those described in Fig. 44-50, except that you are now performing the other way round.

15) Closing Form

As you unbend the legs to rise, the right foot takes a step to the rear. The right hand simultaneously moves to the front of the abdomen. You thus form a left three-in-one posture with your weight mainly on the rear leg. Now, you can either proceed to other exercises or finish with this exercise. If you want to cease practising, you can follow these directions: Bring the left foot next to the right one and unbend the knees to stand up naturally. Lower both arms to the sides of the body in the meantime. Look horizontally forward.

A Practical Example of Dragon Form

If the opponent thrusts his fist into your chest, you can make a grab at his wrist and pull his arms down with your right hand, and chop at his shoulder with your left palm. Meanwhile, you can raise your right foot to tread on his front shin. (Fig. 51)

2. Tiger Exercise

Tigers are the king of all beasts and are famous for their prowess and strength. The movements of tiger exercise just reflect the might and irresistible momentum of a tiger leaping over a ravine or springing on its prey.

The footwork applied in this exercise is similar to that of the Cannon Fist of the Five- element Boxing. The legs take turns to step forward in zigzags. You should make a swift and giant stride without lifting the foot too high off the ground, and then take a firm stance. The technique of the upper limb is series of forward swatting, backward drawing and upward drilling. As the swatting is very much similar to the movement of a tiger pouncing on its prey, this form is called "tiger pouncing".

Tiger exercise puts stress on the strength development. While in practice, you should concentrate your attention, guide your energy stream down to "dantian" and accumulate strength in the body with the shoulders and the waist relaxed so that you can thrust both palms out swiftly and vigorously with a thunderous roar, just like a tiger dashing out of a forest, therefore strike the opponent out in a twinkling.

1) Opening Form

(52)
Take a left three-in-one posture to begin with the following forms.

2) Tiger Form-Left

(53-57)
As the right foot takes a giant step to the front-right, the hands together stretch to the upper-front. As you shift your weight onto the right leg with the knee slightly bent, the left foot goes along, suspending beside the right ankle. You thus form a right one-leg stance. At the same time, both hands make a grab and draw downward and backward to the front of the abdomen with the forearms tightly against the flanks and the centres of the fists facing upward.

(58-61)
As you turn your torso slightly to the left, the left foot takes a giant step to the front-left. The right foot immediately follows up with half a step to form a left three-in-one stance. At the same time, the fists together drill up to the front of the chest. Then, with the forearms rotated inward and the fists changed into palms, both hands abruptly swat from before the mouth to the front at shoulder level (thrusting out and pressing a

little down at the end of the motion), the elbow slightly bent, the arches between the thumb and the forefinger facing each other and the hollows of the hands facing the lower-front. Keep your head erect, shoulders and elbows lowered, waist down and knees strengthened. Look straight ahead.

Points to remember:

The movements of the arms and the steps must synchronize perfectly. Both hands should move in an arc but not in a straight line.

4

3) Tiger Form-Right

(62-65)

As the left foot takes a step to the front-left, the hands together stretch to the upper-front. As you shift your weight onto the left leg with the knee slightly bent, the right foot goes along, suspending beside the left ankle. You thus form a left one-leg stance. At the same time, both hands make a grab and draw downward and backward to the front of the abdomen with the forearms tightly against the flanks and the centres of the fists facing upward.

(66-68)

As you turn your torso slightly to the right, the right foot takes a giant step to the front-right.

59

The left foot immediately follows up with half a step to form a right three-in-one stance. At the same time, the fists together drill up to the front of the chest. Then, with the forearms rotated inward and the fists changed into palms, both hands abruptly swat from before the mouth to the front at shoulder level, the elbow slightly bent, the arches between the thumb and the forefinger fac-ing each other and the hollows of the hands fac-ing the lower-front. Look straight ahead.

4) Tiger Form-Left

(69-72)

As the right foot takes a step to the front-right, the hands together stretch to the upper-front. As

you shift your weight onto the right leg with the knee slightly bent, the left foot goes along, sus-pending beside the right ankle. You thus form a right one-leg stance. At the same time, both hands make a grab and draw downward and backward to the front of the abdomen with the forearms tightly against the flanks and the centres of the fists facing upward.

(73-75)

As you turn your torso slightly to the left, the left foot takes a giant step to the front-left. The right foot immediately follows up with half a step to form a left three-in-one stance. At the same time, the fists together drill up to the front of the chest. Then, with the forearms rotated inward and the fists changed into palms, both hands

the right foot takes a giant step to the front-right. The left foot immediately follows up with half a step to form a right three-in-one stance. At the same time, the fists together drill up to the front of the chest. Then, with the forearms rotated inward and the fists changed into palms, both hands abruptly swat from before the mouth to the front at shoulder level, the elbow slightly bent, the arches between the thumb and the forefinger facing each other and the hollows of the hands facing the lower-front. Look straight ahead.

abruptly swat from before the mouth to the front at shoulder level, the elbow slightly bent, the arches between the thumb and the forefinger facing each other and the hollows of the hands facing the lower-front. Look straight ahead.

5) Turning Form

(76)
Turn your body about 180 degrees to the right with the toes of the right foot swung outward and those of the left one inward. Along with the turn of the body, both arms swing horizontally round.

6) Tiger Form - Right

(77-80)
As the left foot takes a giant step to the front-left, the hands together stretch to the upper-front. As you shift your weight onto the left leg with the knee slightly bent, the right foot goes along, suspending beside the left ankle. You thus form a left one-leg stance. At the same time, both hands make a grab and draw downward and backward to the front of the abdomen with the forearms tightly against the flanks and the centres of the fists facing upward.

(81-83)
As you turn your torso slightly to the right,

7) tiger Form - Left

The same as those described in Fig. 69-75, except that you are now performing the other way round.

8) Tiger Form - Right

The same as those described in Fig. 62-68, except that you are now performing the other way round.

9) Turning Form

Turn your body about 180 degrees to the left with the toes of the left foot swung outward and those of the right one inward. Along with the turn of the body, both arms swing horizontally round.

10) Tiger Form - Left

The same as those described in Fig. 53-61.

11) Closing Form

Now, you can either proceed to other exercises or finish with this one. If you want to cease practising, you can follow these directions: Bring the left foot next to the right one and unbend the knees to stand up naturally. Lower both arms to the sides of the body in the meantime. Look horizontally forward.

A Practical Example of Tiger Form

You can launch a "Tiger Pouncing" to strike your enemy at the chest in due course. (Fig. 84)

3. Monkey Exercise

Monkeys are agile animals living in jungles and high mountains. As the most active one of the twelve, monkey exercise embodies the nimbleness, swiftness and mischievousness of a monkey, and imitates its typical behaviour such as dodging, stretching, rising and shifting. As for footwork, round step, toes-in step, toes-out step, skipping step and hopping step are most frequently used. The hand technique includes catching, hook grasping, crooking, snatching, parrying, outward reaching, swatting and so on.

Monkey exercise especially focuses on agility development of the eyes, the limbs and the trunk. The movements are also full of meaning of attack and defence. You can press close to the opponent and bring him under your control with various methods such as grasping and locking. You can also retreat freely to protect yourself in case the opponent may use a loophole in your defence. You usually make a feint to the east and attack in the west, and strike a blow from bottom to top, aiming mainly at the opponent's crotch, ribs, eyes, throat or head. When you contract the body and withdraw the hands, you should keep your elbows from going far off the chest and the abdomen so as to form close protection.

The crisscross route of the monkey exercise is shown below. You are required to repeat some movements in different directions.

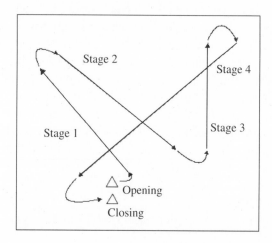

Stage One

1) Opening Form

(85)

Take a left three-in-one posture to begin with the following forms.

2) Monkey Hangs Seal after Left Turn

(86-92)

As you turn your torso slightly to the right, the left foot moves close to the right ankle with the sole off the ground, and then takes a step to

4

the front-left with the toes turned outward. As you then turn your torso to the left, the right foot goes along, resting on the ground next to the left one with the knee bent. At the same time, the left hand swings downward with the forearm rotating inward, then goes rightward and upward with the hollow of the hand turned up, and finally pushes outward and downward with the

hollow of the hand turned out. When the right foot goes forth, the right hand rises to the front of the chest.

(93-94)

The left foot takes a step to the rear to form a right bow stance. At the same time, the right hand continues to stretch forward and upward to eye

level, the elbow bent and the hollow of the hand facing the lower-front. Simultaneously, the left hand withdraws to the front of the abdomen, the hollow of the hand facing downward. Look straight ahead.

Points to remember:

The circling of the left hand must be carried out continuously and be well coordinated with the round step of the left foot. Likewise, the forward stretch of the right hand and the backward step of the left foot must synchronize perfectly. Eyes first follow the left palm and then fix on the right hand. Relax your waist throughout the whole movement.

3) Monkey Holds Rope in the Mouth

(95)

As you turn your torso slightly to the left and shift your weight onto the left leg with the knee bent, the right foot swiftly moves backward, the ball of the foot resting on the ground next to the left one. At the same time, the right hand swings to the front of the crotch, the hollow of the hand facing the right; while the left hand stretches to the upper-right, pausing just before the right cheek, the hollow of the hand facing the right.

Points to remember:

You should contract the body nimbly with the

chest slightly drawn in. The downward swing of the right hand and the upward stretch of the left hand must synchronize perfectly.

4) Monkey Climbs Pole

(96-97)

As you turn your torso slightly to the right, the right foot takes a step forward. At the same time, the left hand presses to the front of the abdomen, the hollow of the hand facing downward; while the right hand rises and then stretches from above the left hand to the front at eye level. Look straight ahead.

(98-102)

The left foot takes a giant step forward. As you shift your weight forward, the right leg swings upward with the knee bent. You thus jump up with the left foot pushing off the ground forcibly. At the same time, the right hand first presses to the front of the abdomen, and then stretches

to the upper- front; while the left hand first stretches to the upper-front, and then presses to the front of the abdomen.

(103-104)

The right hand presses down; while the left hand stretches to the upper-front.

(105-106)

After landing with the left foot, the right foot takes a step forward. As you inclines forth with the right knee bent and the left leg straightened to form a right bow stance, the right hand stretches forward to eye level, the hollow of the hand facing the lower-front; while the left hand presses down, pausing before the abdomen with the hollow of the hand facing downward. Look straight ahead.

Points to remember:

You should perform the whole movement swiftly and continuously without any break. You

4

should jump as high and long as possible, and then take a firm stance. You should act just like an agile monkey climbing up a pole with the hands doing the pressing and stretching alternately along circular paths for five times in all.

Stage Two

5) Monkey Hangs Seal after Right Turn

(107-113)

As you turn your torso slightly to the left, the right foot moves   close to the left ankle with the sole off the ground, and then takes a step to the front-right with the toes turned outward. As you then turn about 180 degrees to the right, the left

foot swings round, resting on the ground next to the right one with the knee bent. At the same time, the right hand swings downward with the forearm rotating inward, then goes leftward and upward with the hollow of the hand turned up, and finally pushes outward and downward with the hollow of the hand turned out. When the left foot goes round, the left hand rises to the front

of the chest.

(114)

The right foot takes a step to the rear to form a left bow stance. At the same time, the left hand continues to stretch forward and upward to eye level, the elbow slightly bent and the hollow of the hand facing the lower-front. Simultaneously,

the right hand withdraws to the front of the abdomen, the hollow of the hand facing downward. Look straight ahead.

6) Monkey Holds Rope in the Mouth

(115)

As you turn your torso slightly to the right and shift your weight onto the right leg with the knee bent, the left foot swiftly moves backward, the ball of the foot resting on the ground next to the right one. At the same time, the left hand swing to the front of the crotch, the hollow of the hand facing the left; while the right hand stretches to the upper-left, pausing just before

66

the left cheek, the hollow of the hand facing the left.

7) Monkey Climbs Pole

(116-118)

As you turn your torso slightly to the left, the left foot takes a step forward. At the same time, the right hand presses to the front of the abdomen, the hollow of the hand facing downward; while the left hand rises and then stretches from above the right hand to the front at eye level. Look straight ahead.

(119-122)

The right foot takes a giant step forward. As you shift your weight forward, the left leg swings upward with the knee bent. You thus jump up with the right foot pushing off the ground forcibly. At the same time, the left hand first presses to the front of the abdomen, and then stretches to the upper-front; while the right hand first stretches to the upper-front, and then presses to the front of the abdomen.

(123-124)

The left hand presses down; while the right

4

hand stretches to the upper-front.

(125-126)

After landing with the right foot, the left foot takes a step forward. As you inclines forth with the left knee bent and the right leg straightened to form a left bow stance, the left hand stretches forward to eye level, the hollow of the hand facing the lower-front; while the right hand presses down, pausing before the abdomen with the hollow of the hand facing downward. Look straight ahead.

Stage Three

8) Monkey Hangs Seal after

Left Turn

(127-132)

As you turn your torso slightly to the right, the left foot moves close to the right ankle with the sole off the ground, and then takes a step to the front-left with the toes turned outward. As you then turn about 180 degrees to the left, the right foot swings round, resting on the ground next to the left one with the knee bent. At the same time, the left hand swings downward with the forearm rotating inward, then goes rightward and upward with the hollow of the hand turned up, and finally pushes outward and downward with the hollow of the hand turned out.

When the right foot goes round, the right hand rises to the front of the chest.

(133)

The left foot takes a step to the rear to form a right bow stance. At the same time, the right hand continues to stretch forward and upward to eye level, the elbow slightly bent and the hollow of the hand facing the lower-front. Simultaneously, the left hand withdraws to the front of the abdomen, the hollow of the hand facing downward. Look straight ahead.

9) Monkey Holds Rope in the Mouth

4

(134)

The same as those described in Fig. 95.

10) Monkey Climbs Pole

(135-145)

The same as those described in Fig. 96-106.

Stage Four

11) Monkey Hangs Seal after Right Turn

The same as those described in Fig. 107-114.

69

12) Monkey Holds Rope in the Mouth

The same as those described in Fig. 115.

13) Monkey Climbs Pole

The same as those described in Fig. 116-126.

14) Closing Form

(146)
The right foot takes a step forward. You then turn round to the left and form a left three-in-one posture with your weight mainly on the right leg. Now, you can either proceed to other exercises or finish with this one. If you want to cease practising, you can follow these directions: Bring the left foot next to the right one and unbend the knees to stand up naturally. Lower both arms to the sides of the body in the meantime. Look horizontally forward.

A Practical Example of Monkey Form

If the opponent thrusts his fist into your chest, you can take a round step and ward off the blow

with one of your hand, and thrust the other hand directly into his face. (Fig. 147)

4. Horse Exercise

Horses are celebrated for there valor and tenacity. In theories of Xingyiquan, horses are highly appraised for their great valiantness to charge and shatter enemy positions. The horse exercise just manifests the momentum of a horse galloping forward. There are two ways concerning this exercise, namely "the single horse form" and "the double horse form". The former, with the fists punching one after the other, has the advantage of two fists assisting each other; while the latter, with the fists dashing together, conduces to a better exertion of integrated strength. The following forms are the former kind, but you do not need to stick to one pattern in practice.

1) Opening Form

(148)

Take a left three-in-one posture to begin with the following forms.

2) Horse Form - Right

(149-151)

As the right hand clenches tight, the left hand makes a grab and draws downward and backward to the front of the abdomen.

(152-154)

The left foot steps forward. Then, shift your

weight completely onto the left leg with the knee slightly bent. The right foot immediately goes along, suspending beside the left ankle. At the same time, the left fist rises with the forearm close against the ribs and the centre of the fist turned up, then drills from before the chin to the front at nose level, the centre of the fist facing obliquely upward; while the right fist follows to the front of the chest with the centre of the fist

turned up.

(155-157)

After a short pause, the right foot swiftly takes a giant step forward. The left foot immediately follows up with half a step to form a right three-in-one stance. At the same time, the right fist thrusts forward with great dashing force from under the left arm, the centre of the fist abruptly

turning down when the fist passes by the left one, the elbow slightly bent. Meanwhile, the left fist withdraws to the front of the chest beside the right upper arm, the elbow bent and the centre of the fist turned down.

Points to remember:

When the right fist thrusts forward, the left fist must draw back to the utmost so as to promote power in the right punch. You should step steadily and take a firm stance, keeping your head erect and shoulders lowered throughout the whole movement.

3) Horse Form - Left

(158-160)

The right foot steps forward. Then, shift your weight completely onto the right leg with the knee slightly bent. The left foot immediately goes along, suspending beside the right ankle. Along with the advance of the body, the right fist withdraws a little and then drills straight ahead to nose level with the centre of the fist turned up.

(161-163)

After a short pause, the left foot swiftly takes a giant step forward. The right foot immediately follows up with half a step to form a left three-in-one stance. At the same time, the left fist thrusts forward with great dashing force from under the right arm, the centre of the fist abruptly turning down when the fist passes by the right one, the elbow slightly bent. Meanwhile, the right

fist withdraws to the front of the chest beside the left upper arm, the elbow bent and the centre of the fist turned down.

Points to remember:

The drill of the right fist must be well coordinated with the forward step of the right foot so as to make full use of the momentum created

from the stride. Likewise, the thrust of the left fist must be in perfect harmony with the step of the left foot and the twist of the waist in order to exert integrated strength.

4) Horse Form - Right

(164-166)

The left foot steps forward. Then, shift your weight completely onto the left leg with the knee slightly bent. The right foot immediately goes along, suspending beside the left ankle. Along with the advance of the body, the left fist withdraws a little and then drills straight ahead to nose level with the centre of the fist turned up.

(167-169)

After a short pause, the right foot swiftly takes a giant step forward. The left foot immediately follows up with half a step to form a right three-in-one stance. At the same time, the right fist thrusts forward with great dashing force from under the left arm, the centre of the fist abruptly turning down when the fist passes by the left one, the elbow slightly bent. Meanwhile, the left fist withdraws to the front of the chest beside the right upper arm, the elbow bent and the centre of the fist turned down.

5) Horse Form - Left

(170-174)

The same as those described in Fig. 158-163.

6) Turning Form

(175-176)

Turn your body about 180 degrees to the right with the toes of the left foot swung inward and those of the right one outward. You thus form a right three-in-one stance with your weight mainly on the left leg. Along with the turn of the body, both arms sweep horizontally round, the right fist reaching forward with the elbow slightly bent, while the left fist moving backward to the front of the chest beside the right upper arm with the elbow bent.

Points to remember:

The horizontal sweep of the arms must be performed swiftly and vigorously, and be well coordinated with the turn of the body.

7) Horse Form - Left

The same as those described in Fig. 158-163, except that you are now performing the other way round.

8) Horse Form - Right

The same as those described in Fig. 164-169, except that you are now performing the other way round.

9) Turning Form

The same as those described in Fig. 175-176, except that you are now turning round to the left. Substitute "left" for "right" and vice versa.

10) Closing Form

Now, you can either proceed to other exercises or finish with this one. If you want to cease practising, you can follow these directions: Bring the left foot next to the right one and unbend the knees to stand up naturally. Lower both arms to the sides of the body with the fists opened in the meantime. Look horizontally forward.

A Practical Example of Horse Form

If the opponent thrusts his right fist into your chest, you can parry off the attack swiftly with your left arm and thrust your right fist straight into his throat. (Fig. 177)

5. Snake Exercise

Snakes are reptiles which are skilled in twining, spiralling, swallowing and crawling tortuously through grasses and bushes, and

flexible with the head and the tail always helping each other. There was a battle position in ancient times in which troops were deployed in a snakelike array. It was said that such an array would make it impossible for the enemy to do anything. "When the head is being attacked, the tail will help; when the tail is being charged, the head will aid; and when the body is in danger, the head and the tail will both give assistance."

The snake exercise takes meanings from the movements of snakes. Your hands should act like a snake's head or tail, and your arms should move like a snake's body. While in practice, you should strive to handle your limbs and trunk nimbly, synchronize your upper and lower halves, and keep a perfect conformity of the internal and the external. You are usually required to make a stretch after huddling yourself up. You should perform movements of opening, closing, spitting and swallowing in lively rhythm, with both hands assisting each other and all parts of the body linked up to exert integrated strength.

Before a snake launches a charge, it usually remains still in order to subdue the enemy by an abrupt attack when it sees a loophole. It is very hard to guard against such an offensive which the snake exercise just mimics. For example, you can make a grab at your opponent like a snake holding a firm grip on its prey, and then step swiftly toward under the opponent's crotch and lean forward against him with great strength, forcing him to fall. The movements of snake exercise are very simple, but it is still necessary for you to practise it again and again so as to see what is behind it.

1) Opening Form

(178)
Take a left three-in-one posture to begin with the following forms.

2) Snake Form - Right

(179-181)
The left foot steps forward with the toes turned outward. As you turn your torso slightly to the left and shift your weight onto the left leg with the knee half bent, the right foot goes along, resting on the ground beside the left one with the heel lifted. At the same, the left hand swings upward and rightward, pausing just above the right shoulder with the elbow bent, the hollow of the hand facing the right and the fingers pointing upward; while the right hand changes into a fist and stretches down, pausing beside the inner side the of the left thigh, the forearm rotated inward, the little finger side of the fist facing the front. Look straight ahead.

75

(182-184)

After a short pause, as you turn your torso slightly to the right, the right foot takes a giant and powerful step forward. The left foot immediately follows up with half a step to form a right three-in-one stance. At the same time, with the arm rotating outward, the right fist swings for-

ward to shoulder level, the eye of the fist on top, the force concentrated on the forearm; while the left hand pulls down, then changes into a fist and withdraws to the left side of the waist with the centre of the fist close against the body. Look straight ahead.

Points to remember:

At the beginning of this form, the movements of the arms must be well coordinated with the forward step of the left foot. You should hold the arms close against the body, bring the shoulders a little forth, draw the chest slightly inward and guide your energy stream down. Then, you should wield the right fist forward swiftly and vigorously, making full use of the momentum

created through the steps and the twist of the torso.

3) Snake Form - Left

(185-187)

The right foot steps forward with the toes turned outward. As you turn your torso slightly

to the right and shift your weight onto the right leg with the knee half bent, the left foot goes along, resting on the ground beside the right one with the heel lifted. At the same time, the right fist changes into a palm and swings upward and leftward, pausing just above the left shoulder with the elbow bent, the hollow of the hand facing the left and the fingers pointing upward; while the left fist stretches down, pausing beside the inner side of the right thigh, the forearm rotated inward, the little finger side of the fist facing the front. Look straight ahead.

(188-190)

After a short pause, as you turn your torso slightly to the left, the left foot takes a giant and powerful step forward. The right foot immediately follows up with half a step to form a left three-in-one stance. At the same time, with the arm rotating outward, the left fist swings forward to shoulder level, the eye of the fist on top, the force concentrated on the forearm; while the right hand pulls down, then changes into a fist and withdraws to the right side of the waist with the centre of the fist close against the body. Look straight ahead.

4) Snake Form - Right

The same as those described in Fig. 185-190. You only need to substitute "left" for "right" and vice versa.

5) Snake Form - Left

The same as those described in Fig. 185-190.

6) Turning Form

(191)

Turn your body about 180 degrees to the right with the toes of the left foot swung inward and those of the right one outward. Along with the turn of the body, the left fist swings close to the chest with the elbow bent; while the right fist moves to the front of the abdomen.

(192-194)

Without any pause, the right foot steps forward. The left foot immediately follows up with half a step to form a right three-in-one stance. At the same time, the right fist swings forward to shoulder level with the eye of the fist on top; while the left fist continues to press down, pausing with the centre of the fist close against the left side of the waist.

7) Snake Form - Left

The same as those described in Fig. 185-190, except that you are now performing the other way round.

8) Snake Form - Right

The same as those described in Fig. 185-190. But you are now performing the other way round, and you need to substitute "left" for "right" and vice versa.

9) Turning Form

The same as those described in Fig. 191-194, except that you are now turning to the left. Substitute "left" for "right" and vice versa.

10) Closing Form

Now, you can either proceed to other exercises or finish with this one. If you want to cease practising, you can follow these directions: Bring the left foot next to the right one and unbend the knees to stand up naturally. Lower both arms to the sides of the body with the fists opened in the meantime. Look horizontally forward.

A Practical Example of Snake Form

If the opponent thrusts his left fist into your chest, you can make a grab at his wrist with your left hand, and step straight ahead with your right foot and swing your right fist forward so as to knock him out. (Fig. 195)

6. Cock Exercise

Cocks are bellicose and good at pecking. The cock exercise just mimics the typical actions of a cock and manifests the accuracy, steadiness, robustness, nimbleness, virility and valiantness of its various behavior. It is an excellent drill for flexibility and harmoniousness development. The movements of "Golden Cock pecks at Rice" should be performed swiftly and accurately, with the upper and the lower limbs in perfect harmony so as to exert integrated strength. While carrying out "Golden Cock Ruffles Feathers", you should take a firm stance and generate vigorous shaking force from your waist. And when you come to "Golden Cock Stands on Single Leg", you should act just like a cock running at top speed and then coming to a sudden halt when it hears something strange. Other forms such as "Golden Cock Perches on High Frame", "Golden Cock Crows at Dawn" and "Golden Cock Spreads Wings" also contain movements of stretching, contracting, turning, jumping and balancing, and can bring benefit to every part of the body.

The cock exercise has a somewhat heavier work load and can help to build up your health in an all-round way. You are usually required to perform the forms of this exercise to and fro along a straight line.

1) Opening Form

(196)
Take a left three-in-one posture to begin with the following forms.

2) Golden Cock Spreads Wings

(197-199)
The left foot steps to the front-left. As you turn your torso to the left and lean a little forth, shift your weight forward with the left knee bent, the right leg straightened and its heel lifted. At

the same time, the right hand stretches from under the left arm to the front at chest level, the hollow of the hand facing the lower-front; while the left hand withdraws to the left side of the waist, the hollow of the hand facing downward. Set your eyes toward the right hand.

Points to remember:

The forward stretch of the right hand and the withdrawal of the left hand must synchronize perfectly. Twist your waist with the right shoulder pushing forth when the right hand reaches out. You do not need to perform this form at high speed.

4

3) Golden Cock Stands on Single Leg

(200-203)

The right foot goes forth, passing beside the left one, and then skips to the front-right. As you shift your weight completely onto the right leg with the knee bent, the left foot follows along, suspending beside the right ankle. You thus form a right one-leg stance. At the same time, the left hand stretches from under the right arm to the front at chest level, the hollow of the hand facing the lower-front; while the right hand withdraws to the right side of the waist, the hollow of the hand facing downward. Set your eyes toward the left hand.

Points to remember:

You should take a giant and quick leap without jumping high off the ground. Then, you should make a firm stand on the right foot, keeping the head erect and the waist down. Concentrate your attention throughout the movement.

4) Golden Cock Spreads Wings

(204-205)

The same as those described in Fig. 197-199.

5) Golden Cock Stands on Single Leg

(206-210)

The same as those described in Fig. 200-203.

you shift your weight onto the right leg with the knee bent, the left foot follows along, suspending beside the right ankle.

6) Golden Cock Pecks at Rice

(211-216)

The left foot takes a step to the front-left. The right foot then goes forth, passing beside the left one, and continues to step to the front-right. As

4

(217-220)

After a short pause, the left foot takes a step to the front-left. The right foot then goes forth, passing beside the left one, and continues to step to the front-right.

(221-224)

The left foot takes a step to the front-left. As you shift your weight onto the left leg with the knee bent, the right foot follows along and then stamps on the ground next to the left one with great strength. At the same time, the right hand changes into a fist and punches straight ahead, the elbow slightly bent and the eye of the fist on step; while the left hand withdraws to the crook of the right arm with the fingers pointing up-

ward. Set your eyes toward the right fist.

Points to remember:

You should advance with brisk and giant strides and in zigzags. Do not lift the body one moment and lower it the next. The position of the upper limbs remains unchanged while you take the first five steps. At the end of the move-ment, the punch of the right fist and the stamp of the right foot must synchronize perfectly.

7) Golden Cock Ruffles Feathers

(225-226)

The right foot takes a step to the rear. Then, turn your torso about 90 degrees to the right and

4

bent both knees to form a left semi-horse-riding stance with your weight mainly on the right leg. At the same time, the right fist changes into a palm and goes to the front-right of the forehead with the elbow bent and raised, the forearm ro-tated inward, and the hollow of the hand facing obliquely outward. Meanwhile, the left hand presses to the lower-left powerfully, pausing outside the left knee with the elbow slightly bent, the hollow of the hand facing the left and the fingers pointing obliquely downward. Set your eyes toward the left hand.

Points to remember:

The movements of the arms and the forming of the stance must synchronize perfectly. When

you separate the arms, you should twist your waist so as to exert shaking force. See that you hold the head erect, the waist down, and the arms well rounded.

8) Golden Cock Perches on High Frame

(227-232)

Turn your torso about 90 degrees to the right with the toes of the right foot swung a little outward. The left foot then takes a step forward. As you shift your weight completely onto the left leg with the knee bent, the right foot follows along, suspending beside the left ankle. You thus

form a left one-leg stance. At the same time, the right hand thrusts straight down, the hollow of the hand just facing the left knee; while the left hand swings upward and rightward, pausing above the right shoulder with the elbow bent, the hollow of the hand facing the right and the fingers pointing to the rear. Look straight ahead.

Points to remember:

You should advance with a giant stride and then make a firm stand on the left foot. The downward thrust of the right hand, the upward swing of the left hand and the forward movement of the right leg must synchronize perfectly.

9) Golden Cock Crows at Dawn

(233-235)

As the left foot pushes the ground forcibly, the right foot takes a step as far ahead as possible. The left foot immediately follows up with half a step to form a right three-in-one stance. At the same time, the right hand swings forward and upward to eye level, the elbow slightly bent and the force concentrated on the forearm; while the left hand presses down to the side of the left hip, the hollow of the hand facing downward. Look straight ahead.

Points to remember:

You should advance with a giant stride so as to generate great impulsive force. The movements of both the hands should be well coordinated with the forward step of the right foot. Hold your head erect and keep the shoulders lowered.

10) Left Chop in Forward Step

(236-237)

The right hand makes a grab and draws down to the front of the abdomen. The left hand changes into a fist in the meantime.

(238-241)

The right foot steps forward. As you shift your weight completely onto the right leg with the knee bent, the left foot follows along, suspending beside the right ankle. At the same time, the right fist rises, and then drills from before the chin to the front, the elbow slightly bent, the centre of the fist facing obliquely upward, and the second joint of the little finger in a straight line just ahead of the tip of the nose.

(242-244)

After a short pause, the left foot steps to the front. The right foot immediately follows up with half a step to form a left three-in-one stance. At the same time, the left fist drills up from before the chest and the chin, then changes into a palm and chops to the front at shoulder level, the elbow slightly bent, the hollow of the hand facing the lower-front and the force concentrated on the base of the palm; while the right fist changes into a palm and withdraws to the right side of the waist, the hollow of the hand facing downward. Set your eyes toward the left hand.

4

11) Right Chop in Forward Step

(245-246)

The left hand makes a grab and draws down to the front of the abdomen. The right hand changes into a fist in the meantime.

(247-250)

The left foot steps forward. As you shift your weight completely onto the left leg with the knee bent, the right foot follows along, suspending beside the left ankle. At the same time, the left fist rises, and then drills from before the chin to the front, the elbow slightly bent, the centre of

the fist facing obliquely upward, and the second joint of the little finger in a straight line just ahead of the tip of the nose.

(251-253)

After a short pause, the right foot steps to the front. The left foot immediately follows up with half a step to form a right three-in-one stance. At

the same time, the right fist drills up from before the chest and the chin, then changes into a palm and chops to the front at shoulder level, the elbow slightly bent, the hollow of the hand facing the lower-front and the force concentrated on the base of the palm; while the left fist changes into a palm and withdraws to the left side of the waist, the hollow of the hand facing downward. Set

your eyes toward the right hand.

12) Stamp and Chop

(254-255)

The right hand makes a grab and draws down to the front of the abdomen. The left hand changes into a fist in the meantime.

(256-257)

As you shift your weight completely onto the left leg and raise the right leg with the knee bent, the right fist drills upward. When it goes past the face, the fist changes into a palm. The left fist simultaneously rises to the front of the chin.

(258-259)

As you bend the left knee to squat yourself a little down, the right foot stamps forcibly on the ground. The left foot immediately goes up, pausing just beside the right calf. You thus form a right one-leg stance. At the same time, the left fist changes into a palm and chops forward and downward to waist level, the hollow of the hand facing the lower-front, the force concentrated on the base of the palm; while the right hand turns over and pulls down, then changes into a fist and withdraws to the right side of the waist. Set your eyes toward the left hand.

Points to remember:

The upward drilling of the right fist and the

rise of the right foot must synchronize perfectly, and so must the chop of the left hand and the stamp of the right foot. Inhale while the right fist goes up and exhale while the left hand chops down so as to promote strength exertion.

13) Golden Cock Pecks at Rice

(260-264)

The left foot takes a step forward. As you shift your weight completely onto the left leg with the knee bent, the right foot follows along, and then stamps on the ground next to the left one. At the same time, the right fist punches straight ahead, the elbow slightly bent and the eye of the

fist on top; while the left hand withdraws to the crook of the right arm with the fingers pointing upward.

Points to remember:

The punch of the right fist must be carried out in cooperation with the stamp of the right foot. You should twist the waist to the left so as

to exert greater strength.

14) Golden Cock Ruffles Feathers

(265-268)

The same as those described in Fig. 225-226,

88

except that you are now performing the other way round.

15) Golden Cock Perches on High Frame

(269-274)

The same as those described in Fig. 227-232,

except that you are now performing the other way round.

16) Golden Cock Crows at Dawn

(275-277)

The same as those described in Fig. 233-235, except that you are now performing the other

4

way round.

17) Closing Form

The right foot takes a step to the rear. At the same time, the left hand stretches forward to shoulder level, while the right hand withdraws to the front of the abdomen. You thus form a left

three-in-one posture with your weight mainly on the right leg. Now, you can either proceed to other exercises or finish with this one. If you want to cease practising, you can follow these directions: Bring the left foot next to the right one and un- bend both knees to stand up naturally. Lower both arms to the sides of the body in the meantime. Look horizontally forward.

A Practical Example of Cock Form

If the opponent thrusts his right fist into your abdomen, you can press the oncoming fist down with your left hand, and step straight ahead with your right foot, swinging your right hand forward and upward to strike him at the chin. (Fig. 278)

7. Swallow Exercise

Swallows are light and spry birds. The swallow exercise is just modeled on the stunt of a swallow skimming over the water, and is composed of leaping, one-leg standing, turning and so on. The movements seem simple but indeed require perfect harmony and dexterousness. While you are performing the "Swallow Skims over Water", you should make a long leap and then take a firm stand, and twist your waist to bring along the arms. You should try to coordinate your upper and lower halves, and keep your will and form in agreement with each other.

1) Opening Form

(279)

Take a left three-in-one posture to begin with the following forms.

2) Swallow Skims over Water

(280-281)

Shift your weight forward and lower the left arm. Both forearms thus get crossed before the abdomen with the left one in front of the right one. Look straight ahead.

(282)

Leap forward with the left foot pushing off the ground and the right foot swinging forth. As you turn your torso slightly to the right, both hands change into fists and rise to head level, and then separate.

(283)

Shift your weight completely onto the right leg with the knee bent. The left foot immediately follows along, suspending beside the right ankle. You thus form a right one-leg stance. Meanwhile, both fists respectively swing sideward down to shoulder level with the elbows

slightly bent, the centres of the fists facing upward and the force concentrated on the backs of the fists. Set your eyes toward the right fist.

Points to remember:

You should leap as far ahead as possible without jumping high off the ground, and then take a firm landing. Keep your head erect and your

waist down. The separation of the arms must be well coordinated with the forming of the one-leg stance.

3) Right Punch in Forward Step

(284-287)

As you turn your torso slightly to the left, the

4

left foot steps forward. The right foot immediately follows up with half a step to form a left three-in-one stance. At the same time, the right fist swings down, passing beside the waist, then punches straight ahead at waist level, the elbow slightly bent and the eye of the fist on top; while the left fist changes into a palm and withdraws, pausing beside the crook of the right arm. Look

straight ahead.

Points to remember:

The punch and the steps must synchronize perfectly. Keep your head erect and your shoulders lowered.

4) Swallow Skims over Water

(288)

Shift your weight forward and lower the left arm. Both forearms thus get crossed before the abdomen with the left one in front of the right one. Look straight ahead.

(289)

Leap forward with the left foot pushing off the ground and the right foot swinging forth. As you turn your torso slightly to the right and clench the left fist, both arms rise to head level and then separate.

(290)

Shift your weight completely onto the right leg with the knee bent. The left foot immediately follows along, suspending beside the right ankle. You thus form a right one-leg stance. Meanwhile, both fists respectively swing sideward down to shoulder level with the elbows slightly bent, the centres of the fists facing up-

ward and the force concentrated on the backs of the fists. Set your eyes toward the right fist.

5) Right Punch in Forward Step

(291-294)

As you turn your torso slightly to the left, the

left foot steps forward. The right foot immediately follows up with half a step to form a left three-in-one stance. At the same time, the right fist swings down, passing beside the waist, then punches straight ahead at waist level, the elbow slightly bent and the eye of the fist on top; while the left fist changes into a palm and withdraws, pausing beside the crook of the right arm. Look straight ahead.

6) Turning Form

(295-297)

Turn your body about 180 degrees to the right and shift your weight onto the left leg with the toes of the left foot swung inward and those of the right one outward. Along with the turn of the body, the right fist swings downward and backward, the force concentrated on the back of the fist.

Points to remember:

The turn of the body and the swing of the right fist must be performed swiftly and smoothly.

7) Swallow Skims over Water

(298)

Leap forward with the left foot pushing off the ground and the right foot swinging forth. As you turn your torso slightly to the right, the right fist goes down with the arm rotated inward; while the left hand changes into a fist and stretches to the right. Both arms thus get crossed in front of the torso with the right one behind the left one.

4

(299-300)

Shift your weight completely onto the right leg with the knee bent. The left foot immediately follows along, suspending beside the right ankle. You thus form a right one-leg stance. Meanwhile, both fists rise to head level, then separate, and respectively swing sideward down to shoulder level with the elbows slightly bent,

the centres of the fists facing upward and the force concentrated on the backs of the fists.

8) Right Punch in Forward Step

(301-304)

The same as those described in Fig. 284-287, except that you are now performing the other

way round.

9) Swallow Skims over Water

The same as those described in Fig. 288-290, except that you are now performing the other way round.

10) Right Punch in Forward Step

The same as those described in Fig. 284-287, except that you are now performing the other way round.

11) Turning Form

The same as those described in Fig. 295-297, except that you are now performing the other way round.

12) Swallow Skims over Water

The same as those described in Fig. 298-300, except that you are now performing the other way round.

13) Right Punch in Forward Step

The same as those described in Fig. 284-287.

14) Closing Form

As you turn your torso slightly to the right, the left hand stretches forward to shoulder level with the hollow of the hand facing the lower-front; while the right fist changes into a palm and withdraws to the front of the abdomen with the hollow of the hand facing downward. Now, you can either proceed to other exercises or finish with this one. If you want to cease practising, you can follow these directions: Bring the left foot next to the right one and unbend both knees to stand up naturally. Lower both arms to the sides of the body in the meantime. Look horizontally forward.

A Practical Example of Swallow Form

If the opponent thrusts his right fist into your head, you can raise your crossed arms to block the blow, then step forward and wield your fist to smash him on the face. (Fig. 305-306)

4

8. Sparrow Hawk Exercise

Sparrow hawks are birds of prey, not very big in form but specially fierce and nimble. The sparrow hawk exercise just conveys the meaning of a flying sparrow hawk and places stress on the training of hand and body techniques. It is true that the movements are a bit more complicated than that of the tiger, horse and snake exercises.

Fierceness is what you should first of all achieve. You should wield your arms swiftly to carry out series blows with irresistible momentum. When you thrust the fist out, you should aim at the enemy's heart or mouth, and give consideration to both the attack and the defence just as you do with Cannon Fist.

1) Opening Form

(307)

Take a left three-in-one posture to begin with the following forms.

2) Sparrow Hawk Folds Wings

(308-311)

The right foot takes a step forward. As you shift your weight onto the right leg with the knee slightly bent, the left foot goes along, suspending beside the right ankle. At the same time, clench both your fists. The right fist rises, passing before the chest, then drills from above the left arm to the front at shoulder level, the elbow slightly bent and the centre of the fist facing upward; while the left fist withdraws, resting against the abdomen with the centre of the fist facing downward. Look straight ahead.

Points to remember:

You should advance with a giant stride and then take a firm stand. The step of the right foot

and the drill of the right fist must synchronize perfectly.

3) Sparrow Hawk Flies into Woods

(312-313)

The left foot steps forward. The right foot immediately follows up with half a step. You thus

form a left semi-horse-riding stance with both knees bent and your weight mainly on the right leg. At the same time, the left fist thrusts forward to shoulder level, the elbow slightly bent and the eye of the fist on top; while the right fist moves rightward and a little upward, pausing just before the forehead with the elbow bent, the forearm rotated inward and the centre of the fist facing outward. Look in the direction of the left fist.

4) Sparrow Hawk Soars into Sky

Points to remember:

The thrust of the left fist and the up-block of the right arm must be well coordinated with the forming of the stance. Press both knees slightly inward, and keep the waist down, the shoulders relaxed and lowered.

(314-318)

The left foot steps forward. As you turn your torso slightly to left, the right foot takes a step to the front. The left foot then follows up with half a step to form a right three-in-one stance. At the same time, with the elbow bent and the forearm

rotated inward, the left fist presses down to the front of the abdomen, the centre of the fist facing downward; while the right fist drops to the side of the waist, then goes up to chest level and finally drills forward to mouth level, the elbow slightly bent and the centre of the fist facing upward. Look straight ahead.

Points to remember:

You should apply wrapping force to the right arm when it goes down and keep the forearm close against the flank when the right fist rises. The drill of the right fist should be carried out swiftly and vigorously, and be well coordinated with the steps.

97

5) Turning Form

(319-322)

As you turn about 180 degrees to the left with the toes of the right foot swung inward and those of the left one outward, the right arm sweeps horizontally round.

(323-324)

The left foot steps forward. The right foot immediately follows up with half a step to form a left three-in-one stance. At the same time, the left fist rises, and then drills forward from above the right arm to mouth level, the elbow slightly bent and the centre of the fist facing upward;

while the right fist withdraws to the right side of the waist.

Points to remember:

You should turn round swiftly and smoothly, exerting great strength through the sweeping right arm without the least slackness. The drill of the left fist and the step of the left foot must

synchronize perfectly.

6) Sparrow Hawk Flips Over

(325)

As you shift you weight slightly leftward, the left fist goes close to the chest with the elbow bent and the forearm rotated inward. Meanwhile,

the right fist rises from outside the left elbow, the centre of the fist facing the body.

(326)

Turn your torso to the right and shift your weight toward the right leg as you straighten the left leg. At the same time, the right fist continues to move upward, pausing just before the forehead with the elbow bent and raised, the centre of the fist facing outward; while the left fist drops, the eye of the fist facing downward.

(327-328)

As you further bend the knees to lower the body, the left fist continues to stretch down along the inner side of the left leg. When the left fist goes past the left knee, turn your torso swiftly to the left and shift your weight a little forward to form a left semi-horse-riding stance. The left fist then continues to stretch forward and stick up abruptly, the arm rotated outward, the elbow slightly bent and just above the left knee, the eye of the fist facing upward. The right fist simultaneously drops to the right side of the waist, the centre of the fist facing upward. Look in the direction of the left fist.

Points to remember:

You should twist your torso in response to the smooth and continuous shift of your weight and the movements of the arms.

7) Sparrow Hawk Folds Wings

As you turn your torso about 90 degrees to the left, the right foot takes a step forward. Then, as you shift your weight onto the right leg with the knee slightly bent, the left foot goes along, suspending beside the right ankle. At the same time, the right fist rises, passing before the chest, then drills from above the left arm to the front at shoulder level, the elbow slightly bent and the centre of the fist facing upward; while the left fist withdraws, resting against the abdomen with the centre of the fist facing downward. Look straight ahead. (Refer to Fig. 311, except that you are now facing the opposite direction.)

8) Sparrow Hawk Flies into Woods

The same as those described in Fig. 312-313, except that you are now performing the other way round.

9) Sparrow Hawk Soars into Sky

The same as those described in Fig. 314-318, except that you are now performing the other way round.

10) Turning Form

The same as those described in Fig. 319-324, except that you are now performing the other way round.

11) Sparrow Hawk Flips Over

The same as those described in Fig. 325-328, except that you are now performing the other way round.

12) Closing Form

Now, you can either proceed to other exercises or finish with this on. If you want to cease practising, you can follow these directions: Unbend both legs and bring the left foot next to the right one to stand up naturally. Lower the arms to the sides of the body with the fists opened in the meantime. Look horizontally forward.

A Practical Example of Sparrow Hawk Form

If the opponent thrusts his right fist into your chest, you can intercept the oncoming blow with your left arm, and step straight ahead, thrusting your right fist to hit him at the nose. (Fig. 329)

9. Alligator Exercise

Alligators are large fierce animals like crocodiles that live mainly in lakes and rivers. They can not only move in water nimbly and freely, but also stir up great surges. The alligator exercise is just in pursuit of the movement features of an alligator. You should wield your arms up and down, or stretch one hand forward with the other staying behind, so that you can strictly guard the chest and get ready to launch an attack at any time. You usually advance in zigzags, transferring through one-leg stances. This exercise attaches importance to the twist of the waist. You should coordinate your arms, legs, trunk and eyes, using the waist as the axis to bring along the limbs. You should concentrate your attention, trying to be soft outwardly but strong inwardly, giving a peaceful appearance but accumulating strength inside. The force should be focused on the palms.

1) Opening Form

(330)
Take a left three-in-one posture to begin with the following forms.

2) Alligator Form - Right

(331-335)
The right foot takes a step to the front-right. As you turn your torso slightly to the right and shift your weight onto the right leg with the knee slightly bent, the left foot goes along, suspending beside the right ankle. You thus form a right one-leg stance. At the same time, the right hand rises to mouth level with the hollow of the hand facing upward, then turns over and moves a little forward; while the left hand swings downward, inward and then upward to the front of the abdomen with the hollow of the hand turned up. Set your eyes on the right palm.

Points to remember:

The circular movements of the arms should be well coordinated with the stride of the right leg. The force must be concentrated on the little finger sides of the palms. You should relax your waist, bring the shoulders a little forth with the chest drawn slightly inward.

3) Alligator Form - Left

(336-339)

The left foot takes a step to the front-left. As you turn your torso slightly to the left and shift your weight onto the left leg with the knee bent, the right foot goes along, suspending beside the left ankle. You thus form a left one-leg stance.

4

At the same time, the left hand rises to mouth level, then turns over and moves a little forward; while the right hand circles forward, downward, inward and then upward to the front of the abdomen with the hollow of the hand turned up. Set your eyes on the left palm.

Points to remember:

Both hands should circle smoothly and harmoniously.

4) Alligator Form - Right

(340-342)

The right foot takes a step to the front-right. As you turn your torso slightly to the right and

shift your weight onto the right leg with the knee bent, the left foot goes along, suspending beside the right ankle. You thus form a right one-leg stance. At the same time, the right hand rises to mouth level, then turns over and moves a little forward; while the left hand circles forward, downward, inward and then upward to the front of the abdomen with the hollow of the hand turned up. Set your eyes on the right palm.

5) Alligator Form - Left

(343-345)

The same as those described in Fig. 336-339.

6) Turning Form

(346-350)

Turn your body about 180 degrees to the right on the ball of the left foot. The right foot then takes a step to the front-right. As you turn your torso slightly to the right and shift your weight onto the right leg with the knee slightly bent, the left foot goes along, suspending beside the right ankle. At the same time, the right hand rises to mouth level, then turns over and moves a little forward; while the left hand circles forward, downward, inward and then upward to the front of the abdomen with the hollow of the hand turned up.

Points to remember:

You should turn round swiftly and steadily and then step forward without any break in between.

7) Alligator Form - Left

The same as those described in Fig. 336-339, except that you are now performing the other way round.

8) Alligator Form - Right

The same as those described in Fig. 340-342, except that you are now performing the other way round.

9) Alligator Form - Left

The same as those described in Fig. 336-339, except that you are now performing the other way round.

10) Turning Form

The same as those described in Fig. 346-350, except that you are now performing the other way round.

11) Closing Form

The left foot takes a step forward. At the same time, the left hand stretches forward to shoulder level with the hollow of the hand facing the lower-front; while the right hand presses down, pausing with the root of the thumb close against the abdomen, the hollow of the hand facing downward. You thus form a left three-in-one posture with your weight mainly on the right leg. Now, you can either proceed to other exercises or finish with this one, If you want to cease practising, you can follow these directions: Bring the left foot next to the right one and unbend both knees to stand up naturally. Lower both arms to the sides of the body in the meantime. Look horizontally forward.

A Practical Example of Alligator Form

If the opponent thrusts his right fist into your chest, you can press his fist down with your left hand, and wield your right hand to strike him at the throat. (Fig. 351)

4

10. Tai Exercise

"Tai" is a fierce ostrich-like animal in ancient Chinese fables. It was said that a "tai" was good at flying upward and was strong enough to smash anything when it dived down.

The movements of the tai exercise are therefore shaped like flying and smashing to improve the coordination of the shoulders, arms, waist and legs, and develop integrated strength of the whole body.

The footwork of tai exercise is similar to that of the tiger exercise, that is to say, you should advance in zigzags. The hand technique

is usually a double dash of fists along with a forward stride after circular swings of the arms.

1) Opening Form

(352)

Take a left three-in one posture to begin with

the following forms.

2) Tai Form - Left

(353-357)

The right foot takes a step to the front-right. As you shift your weight onto the right leg with the knee slightly bent, the left foot goes along,

suspending beside the right ankle. At the same time, the right arm swings to the left, while the left arm drops and swings to the right. Both arms thus get crossed in front of the torso with the right one behind the left one, the hollows of the hands facing downward. Without any pause, both arms rise to the front of the face, then separate. The hands thus swing sideward down, and then withdraw respectively to the sides of the waist, the palms changed into fists and the centres of the fists facing upward.

(358-360)

As you turn your torso slightly to the left, the left foot takes a giant step to the front-left. The right foot immediately follows up with half a step to form a left three-in-one stance. At the same time, the two fists together ram straight ahead, the elbows slightly bent. Look to the front.

Points to remember:

The sideward swings of the arms must be well coordinated with the stride of the right leg and be full of separating force. You should then take a firm stand and keep your balance. You should carry out the double dash with great momentum, and with the elbows brushing against the flanks. Keep your head erect, shoulders lowered, waist down and the knees strengthened in the fixed position.

3) Tai Form - Right

(361-364)

The left foot takes a step to the front-left. As you shift your weight onto the left leg with the knee slightly bent, the right foot goes along, suspending beside the left ankle. At the same time, both arms get crossed in front of the torso with the right one behind the left one, the forearms rotated inward and the fists changed into palms. Without any pause, both arms rise to the front of the face, then separate. The hands thus swing sideward down, and then withdraw respectively to the sides of the waist, the palms changed into fists and the centres of the fists facing upward.

(365-367)

As you turn your torso slightly to the right, the right foot takes a giant step to the front-right. The left foot immediately follows up with half a step to form a right three-in-one stance. At the same time, the two fists together ram straight ahead, the elbows slightly bent. Look to the front.

4) Tai Form - Left

(368-370)

The right foot takes a step to the front-right. As you shift your weight onto the right leg with the knee slightly bent, the left foot goes along, suspending beside the right ankle. At the same time, both arms get crossed in front of the torso with the right one behind the left one, the fore-

105

arms rotated inward and the fists changed into palms. Without any pause, both arms rise to the front of the face, then separate. The hands thus swing sideward down, and then withdraw respectively to the sides of the waist, the palms changed into fists and the centres of the fists facing upward.

(371-373)

As you turn your torso slightly to the left, the left foot takes a giant step to the front-left. The right foot immediately follows up with half a step to form a left three-in-one stance. At the same time, the two fists together ram straight ahead, the elbows slightly bent. Look to the front.

5) Turning Form

(374-375)

Turn your body about 180 degrees to the right with the toes of the right foot swung outward and those of the left one inward. Along with the turn of the body, both arms sweep horizontally

round. You thus form a right three-in-one stance with your weight mainly on the left leg. Look straight ahead.

Points to remember:

You should turn round swiftly and steadily with both elbows pressing against the flanks so as to exert horizontal sweeping force through the

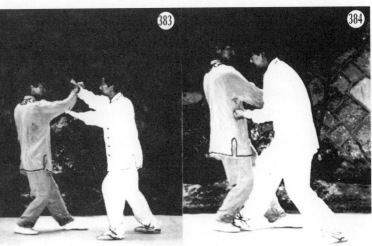

arms. Keep your head erect and guide the energy stream down.

6) Tai Form - Right

(376-382)

The same as those described in Fig. 361-367, except that you are now performing the other way round.

7) Tai Form - Left

The same as those described in Fig. 368-373, except that you are now performing the other way round.

8) Turning Form

The same as those described in Fig. 374-375, except that you are now performing the other way round.

9) Tai Form - Right

The same as those described in Fig. 361-367.

10) Closing Form

The right foot takes a step to the rear. At the same time, open both your fists. The left hand stretches forward to shoulder level with the hol-

low of the hand facing the lower-front; while the right hand withdraws, pausing with the root of the thumb close against the abdomen, the hollow of the hand facing downward. You thus form a left three-in-one posture with your weight mainly on the right leg. Now, you can either proceed to other exercises or finish with this one. If you want to cease practising, you can follow these directions: Bring the left foot next to the right one and unbend both knees to stand up naturally. Lower both arms to the sides of the body in the meantime. Look horizontally forward.

A Practical Example of Tai Exercise

If the opponent thrusts his right fist into your face, you can raise your crossed arms to ward off the blow, and then step forward and thrust both your fists to dash against his abdomen. (Fig. 383-384)

11. Eagle and Bear Exercise

Eagles are sharp-eyed birds of prey, adept in catching. Bears are large beasts of great strength. This exercise is a good combination of two kinds of characteristics, displaying the nimbleness and accuracy of an eagle chasing its prey and the valor and might of a bear coming out of its lair. Therefore, it is commonly called a compound drill of eagle and bear. In particular, the movement of rise must manifest the power of a bear standing up with its head hold upward; and the movement of fall must exhibit the spryness of an eagle snatching its prey with its talons. By practising rising, falling, drilling and overturning, alternating between the left and the right forms, you can effectively train your body in an overall way.

As ancient boxing manuals states, eagle exercise lays stress on relentlessness and bear exercise places emphasis on prowess. The methods of eagle form are locking the opponent's joints and striking him at the chest or belly; while the methods of bear form are guarding your chest with your own arms and striking the opponent at the mouth or nose when you can take advantage of a loophole. When you rise with one fist drilling upward, you should hold your head erect and cast your eyes upward just like a bear fighting against an eagle. When you go down to form a cross-legged stance with the torso twisting to the side, you should make a grab with one hand and do a catch with the other, and cast your eyes downward, just like an eagle swooping down on a bear.

The words "eagle and bear" are a homophone of "hero" in Chinese pronunciation. This also suggests that the indomitable will and spirit that eagles and bears have to fight each other are absolutely necessary for practising Xingyiquan. Therefore, the eagle form and

the bear form are combined into a single exercise.

1) Opening Form

(385)

Take a left three-in-one posture to begin with the following forms.

2) Bear Form - Right Rise

(386-388)

The left foot moves half a step forward. The right foot immediately follows along. As you turn your torso slightly to the left, bend both knees with the heel of the right foot lifted and your

weight distributed evenly on both legs. At the same time, clench both your fists. The right fist drills upward, passing before the left part of the abdomen and the mouth successively, and finally reaches the upper-front-right with the forearm rotated outward, the elbow bent and the centre of the fist facing the rear; while the left fist drops to the left side of the waist. Set your eyes toward the right fist.

Points to remember:

The movements of the arms must be well coordinated with the steps. The right fist must go up along a smooth curve.

3) Eagle Form - Left Fall

(389-390)

Shift your weight completely onto the left leg and raise the right leg with the knee bent. At the same time, the left fist drills up to the front of the face.

(391-392)

The right foot steps to the front-right with the toes turned outward. As you turn your torso to the right and incline forward, bend both knees still further with the heel of the left foot lifted. You thus form a cross-legged semi-squat. At the same time, the left fist stretches forward along the inner side of the right arm. When it goes past the right hand, the fist abruptly changes into a

palm and then presses down, the elbow slightly bent, the hollow of the hand facing the lower-front. In the meantime, the right fist changes into a palm and pulls downward and backward to the side of the right hip, the elbow bent, the hollow of the hand facing the rear. Set your eyes toward the left palm.

Points to remember:

The whole movement must be performed harmoniously like an eagle swooping down on a chick.

4) Bear Form - Left Rise

(393-394)

The right foot moves half a step forward with the toes turned outward. The left foot immediately follows along. Bend both knees with the heel of the left foot lifted and your weight distributed evenly on both legs. At the same time, the left hand makes a grab and draws backward, then drills upward, passing before the right part of the abdomen and the mouth successively, and finally reaches the upper-front-left with the forearm rotated outward, the elbow bent and the centre of the fist facing the rear; while the right hand changes into a fist and moves to the right side of the waist. Set your eyes toward the left fist.

5) Eagle Form - Right Fall

(395-396)

Shift your weight completely onto the right leg and raise the left leg with the knee bent. At the same time, the right fist drills up to the front of the face.

(397-399)

The left foot steps to the front-left with the toes turned outward. The right foot immediately follows along. As you turn your torso to the left and incline forward, bend both knees still further with the heel of the right foot lifted. You thus form a cross-legged semi-squat. At the same time, the right fist continues to stretch upward and forward. When it goes past the left hand, the fist abruptly changes into a palm and then presses down, the elbow slightly bent, the hollow of the hand facing the lower-front. In the meantime, the left fist changes into a palm and pulls downward and backward to the side of the left hip, the elbow bent, the hollow of the hand facing the rear. Set your eyes toward the right palm.

6) Turning Form

(400)

As you unbend both knees to stand up, turn your body to the right with the toes of the left foot swung inward and those of the right one outward. At the same time, clench both your fists. The right fist thus swings close to the chest, the elbow bent and the centre of the fist facing the torso; while the left fist rises to the front of the left shoulder, the elbow raised and the centre of the fist facing downward.

(401-402)

As you continue to turn to the right, the right foot takes a step forward. Along with the turn of the body, the right fist swings downward, passing before the abdomen, then forward to waist level, the force concentrated on the back of the fist. The left fist drops to the left side of the waist in the meantime. Look straight ahead.

Points to remember:

The whole turn is about 180 degrees. The swing of the right fist must be performed swiftly and smoothly, and be well coordinated with the turn of the body.

7) Bear Form - Left Rise

(403-404)

The right foot moves half a step forward with the toes turned outward. The left foot immediately follows along. Bend both knees with the heel of the left foot lifted and your weight distributed evenly on both legs. At the same time,

the left fist drills upward, passing before the right part of the abdomen and the mouth successively, and finally reaches the upper-front-left with the forearm rotated outward, the elbow bent and the centre of the fist facing the rear. The right fist withdraws to the right side of the waist in the meantime. Set your eyes toward the left fist.

8) Eagle Form - Right Fall

(405)
Shift your weight completely onto the right leg and raise the left leg with the knee bent. At the same time, the right fist drills up to the front of the face.

(406-407)
The left foot steps to the front-left with the toes turned outward. The right foot immediately follows along. As you turn your torso to the left and incline forward, bend both knees still further with the heel of the right foot lifted. You thus form a cross-legged semi-squat. At the same time, the right fist continues to stretch upward and forward. When it goes past the left hand, the fist abruptly changes into a palm and then presses down, the elbow slightly bent, the hollow of the hand facing the lower-front. In the meantime, the left fist changes into a palm and pulls downward and backward to the side of the left hip, the elbow bent, the hollow of the hand facing the rear. Set your eyes toward the right palm.

9) Bear Form - Right Rise

The same as those described in Fig. 393-394, except that you are now performing the other way round and with the "left" and the "right" reversed.

10) Eagle Form - Left Fall

The same as those described in Fig. 389-392, except that you are now performing the other way round.

11) Bear Form - Left Rise

The same as those described in Fig. 393-394, except that you are now performing the other way round.

12) Eagle Form - Right Fall

The same as those described in Fig. 395-399, except that you are now performing the other way round.

13) Turning Form

The same as those described in Fig. 400-402, except that you are now performing the other way round.

111

14) Closing Form

The right foot takes a step to the rear. At the same time, open both your fists. The left hand stretches forward to shoulder level with the hollow of the hand facing the lower-front; while the right hand withdraws, pausing with the root of the thumb close against the abdomen, the hollow of the hand facing downward. You thus form a left three-in-one posture with your weight mainly on the right leg. Now, you can either proceed to other exercises or finish with this one. If you want to cease practising, please follow these directions: Bring the left foot next to the right one and unbend both knees to stand up naturally. Lower both arms to the sides of the body in the meantime. Look horizontally forward.

A Practical Example of Eagle and Bear Forms

If the opponent thrusts his right fist into your chest, you can first conduct a "Bear Form - Right Rise" to intercept the blow, and then carry out a "Eagle Form - Left Fall" to bring the opponent under your control. Speaking in detail, you can make a grab at the opponent's right wrist with your right hand, and stretch your left hand to catch him by the right shoulder, then twist the arm and press it down with explosive strength. (Fig. 408-410)

Chapter Five

Shadowboxing Routines

1. Five-element Linked Boxing

The five-element linked boxing is composed in the light of the mutual promotion and restraint among the five elements. Based on the movements of the five-element boxing, this typical routine of Xingyiquan is notable for its well-organized structure, lively style and inexhaustible subtlety.

Usually you are required to practise the five-element linked boxing twice at a time. After you finish with all the forms of the routine, you can start all over again until you return to the original position and conclude the exercise with a closing form. However, you can perform the routine again and again, the number of rounds only depending upon your physical strength.

1) Opening Form

(1)

Stand upright with your head erect, mouth closed with the tongue pushing upward against the hard palate, arms hanging down naturally. Hold the heels together with the tiptoes pointing obliquely outward. Never throw your chest out, nor hump your back. Concentrate your attention and breathe naturally. Look horizontally forward.

(2-4)

Raise both your arms sideways to shoulder level with hollows of the hands facing downward.

(5-7)

Bend both knees to drop to a semi-squat as you turn your torso slightly to the right with the left foot turning on the heel about 45 degrees inward. Meanwhile, clench both your fists and move them inward. Both fists then drop to the front of the abdomen with the forefists facing each other and the centres of the fists facing downward.

(8-10)

As you turn your torso slightly to the left, the right fist rises with the centre of the fist turned up and the forearm closely against the flank, then drills passing from before the chin to the front with the shoulder pushing forth, the elbow slightly bent, the forefist in a spiral and the second joint of the little finger in a straight line just before the tip of the nose.

(11-13)

The left foot takes a big step forward. The right foot immediately follows up with half a step to form a left three-in-one stance. At the same time, with the centre of the fist turned up, the left fist rises, passing before the chest and the

chin, then changes into a palm and chops to the front at shoulder level, the hand cupped with the hollow of the hand facing the lower-front, the forefinger pointing upward and the thumb stretching extremely outward; while the right fist changes into a palm and withdraws until the root of the thumb gets close against the abdomen with the wrist lowered, the hollow of the hand facing downward. Look straight ahead.

Points to remember:

You should perform the above movements slowly and steadily. Hold your torso upright throughout the movements with both shoulders relaxed and lowered. Keep the chest slightly in and the abdomen naturally solidified, but do not

tension the breast or bulge the belly purposely.

2) Right Punch in Forward Step (Black Tiger Comes Out of Lair)

(14-16)

The left foot takes a big step forward. The right foot immediately follows up with half a step. At the same time, clench both your fists. The right fist punches straight ahead at high speed like an arrow with the eye of the fist on top and the forefist inclined forward; while the left fist withdraws to the left side of the waist with the centre of the fist facing upward. Look in the direction of the right fist.

Points to remember:

5

115

You should advance steadily and evenly with your feet moving not far off the ground. The thrust of the right fist must coincide with the landing of the left foot.

3) Crosscut in Backward Step (Blue Dragon Goes Out of Water)

(17-18)

The right foot takes half a step backward. With the left foot moving backward, the left fist goes to the front of the abdomen.

(19-20)

Without any pause, as the left foot continues to move to the rear to form a cross-legged stance, the right fist withdraws to the right side of the waist with the centre of the fist facing upward. Meanwhile, with the forearm rotating outward, the left fist thrusts from beneath the right forearm to the front at shoulder level, the left shoulder pushing forth, the elbow slightly bent and the centre of the fist facing obliquely upward. Look to the front-left.

Points to remember:

Do not change the position of the upper body while the right foot retreats. Shift your weight backward continuously without any break. The thrust of the left fist must coincide with the backward step of the left foot and the twist of the waist so as to exert crosscut strength.

4) Right Punch in Smooth Step (Black Tiger Comes Out of Lair)

(21-22)

The right foot takes a step to the front-right. The left foot immediately follows up with half a step. At the same time, the right fist punches straight ahead in the direction of the right leg with the eye of the fist on top and the forefist inclined slightly forward; while the left fist withdraws to the left side of the waist with the centre of the fist facing upward. Set your eyes on the right fist.

Points to remember:

You should synchronize the punch of the right fist with the step of the right foot. There must not be a break between this form and the former one. When you have neutralized the opponent's blow with your left crosscut fist, you should carry out the right punch promptly to attack the opponent at the belly or ribs.

5) Retreat and Strike Fists Down (White Crane Spreads Wings)

(23)

As you turn your torso to the left and shift

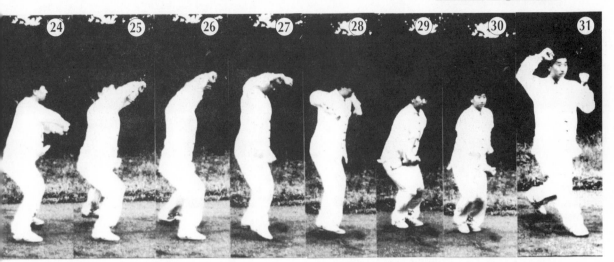

your weight onto the left leg, the left fist stretches to the front of the abdomen. At the same time, with the elbow bent and the forearm rotated inward, the right fist comes back close to the body and then plunges down from outside the left forearm. Both the forearms thus get crossed against the abdomen with the centre of the fists facing backward.

(24-26)

As you shift your weight onto the right leg, raise both your fists to the upper-front of the head, and then separate them.

(27-29)

The left foot takes half a step backward. When the weight is shifted beyond the left leg, both feet together retreat with a stamp, the knees bent and the torso turned slightly to the right. At the same time, both fists drop from the sides respectively, and then strike inward and downward until they get crossed in front of the abdomen, the eyes of the fists facing upward, the left fist nestling against the belly and the right wrist pressing on the left one from out.

Points to remember:

You should coordinate the plunge of the right fist with the left turn of the torso. Then, you should synchronize the strike of the fists and the stamp, exhaling with a sound to promote strength

exertion. When the arms get crossed, hold them closely against the abdomen with the shoulders exerting sinking force as far as possible. Keep the abdomen tight and solidified with your vital energy flowing down to "dantian."

6) Left Cannon

(30-32)

The right foot takes as big a step as possible to the front-right swiftly. The left foot immediately follows up with half a step to form a right three-in-one stance. At the same time, the right fist drills upward, passing before the chest and the face with the centre of the fist facing backward. Then, with the forearm rotating inward, the right fist pushes to the front- right of the forehead, the arm raised and rounded, the center of the fist facing the front. Simultaneously, the left fist thrusts to the front at chest level with the elbow slightly bent and the eye of the fist on top.

Points to remember:

You should coordinate the thrust of the left fist with the landing of the right foot, making full use of the impulsive and twisting force generated with the step and the turn of the torso.

5

7) Cover Elbow and Chop with palm (Black Dragon Draws Water)

(33)

As the right foot takes a step backward, the right arm drops to the front of the chest with the elbow bent and the centre of the fist facing downward. Meanwhile, the left fist goes downward and backward, then rises to the front of the chest with the elbow bent.

(34-35)

Turn your torso to the right and bring the left

foot next to the right one with the toes resting on the ground. At the same time, both fists continue to circle respectively, the right one downward, outward and then upward; while the left one outward, downward and then inward.

(36-38)

Without any pause, as you turn your torso to the left, the left foot takes a step to the front. The right foot immediately follows up with half a step to form a left three-in-one stance. At the same time, the right fist continues to move upward and inward, then changes into a palm and presses down until the root of the thumb gets close against the abdomen with the hollow of the hand facing downward; while the left fist

drills upward, passing before the chest and the chin, then changes into a palm and chops to the front at shoulder level with the elbow slightly bent and the hollow of the hand facing the lower-front. Look straight ahead.

Points to remember:

The circles of the arms should be carried out continuously and coordinated with the twist of the torso. You should apply wrapping strength to the right forearm while it passes from outside the left elbow.

8) Right Drill in Twisted Step (Sparrow Hawk Soars into Sky)

(39-40)

The left foot takes a big step forward. The right foot immediately follows up with half a step to form a left three-in-one stance. At the same time, the right palm changes into a fist and rises passing before the chest and the chin, then drills swiftly to the front, the elbow slightly bent, the centre of the fist facing obliquely upward, the second joint of the little finger in a straight line just before the tip of the nose; while the left palm withdraws until the root of the thumb gets close against the abdomen with the hollow of the hand facing downward.

Points to remember:

You should coordinate the drill of the right fist with the powerful landing of the left foot so as to exert integrated strength.

9) Chop with Palm in Hopping Step (Leopard Cat Climbs a Tree)

(41-42)

The left foot takes a step forward.

(43-44)

As you hop ahead with a tread of the left foot, the right leg swings and kicks forward with the foot hooked, the force concentrated on the heel. At the same time, the left palm first changes into a fist and rises to the front of the chest, then changes back into a palm and chops from before the chin to the front; while the right fist opens and pulls downward and backward.

5

119

(45-46)

On landing, bend the left knee to squat your-self down, and place the right foot to the front with the toes turned outward. Both legs thus get crossed to form a seated stance with the left knee just behind the back of the right knee. Along with the drop of the body, the left palm continues to chop to the lower-front. Look in the direction of the left palm.

Points to remember:

All the movements of this form should be performed swiftly and continuously without any interruption. The kick of the right leg must coincide with the hopping. Keep your balance as you land and squat down.

10) Right Punch in Forward Step (Black Tiger Comes Out of Lair)

(47-48)

Raise your body a little with the right foot taking half a step forward. The left foot immediately rises. Clench both your fists in the meantime.

(49-50)

The left foot takes a big step forward. The right foot immediately follows up with half a step to form a left three-in-one stance. At the same time, the left fist withdraws to the left side of the waist with the centre of the fist facing upward; while the right fist punches straight ahead with the eye of the fist on top. Look in the direction of the right fist.

120

Points to remember:

You should perform the punch with your torso twisting to the left and your right shoulder pushing forth, and concentrate force on the foremost end of the right fist.

11) Left Punch

(51-52)

The left foot takes a step forward. The right foot immediately follows up with half a step. At the same time, the left fist punches straight ahead with the eye of the fist on top; while the right fist withdraws to the right side of the waist with the centre of the fist facing upward. Look in the direction of the left fist.

Points to remember:

You should coordinate the punch of the left fist with the big and swift step of the left foot, finishing them at the same time so as to exert integrated strength.

12) Turning Form (Leopard Cat Backs Up a Tree)

(53-54)

Turn your torso round to the right with the toes of the left foot swung inward. Then, shift your weight back onto the left leg. At the same time, the left fist moves in an arc to the right

with the elbow bent and the forearm rotated inward until it gets close against the abdomen with the center of the fist facing downward. Look horizontally forward.

(55-56)

As you unbend the left leg to stand up, raise your right leg with the knee bent, the foot hooked and the toes turned outward. At the same time, the right fist rises, passing before the chest and the chin, then drills to the front at nose level, the elbow slightly bent and the centre of the fist facing obliquely upward; while the left fist moves a little forward and pauses just beneath the right elbow.

(57-59)

Bend the left knee to squat yourself down and place the right foot to the front with the toes still turned out. You thus form a seated stance with the legs crossed, the left knee just behind the back of the right knee, and the buttocks on the calf of the left leg. At the same time, open both your fists. The left palm rises and then chops to the lower-front; while the right palm turns down and pulls downward and backward to the side of the right hip. Look straight ahead.

Points to remember:

The turn should be carried out continuously without any interruption. The drill of the right fist should coincide with the rise of the right leg

which should have the meaning of treading forward. Keep your balance while you stand on one leg. Finally, you should coordinate the chop of the left palm with the landing of the right foot and the squatting of the body.

Those are the description of a round of the "five-element linked boxing." Now you can practise the above movements all over again, starting with the right foot moving a little forward to initiate the "Right Punch in Forward Step."

13) Closing Form

The right foot takes a step backward. The left foot then moves next to the right one. At the same time, raise both your arms sideways with the hollows of the hands facing upward, and then move the hands inward with the elbows bent. As you slowly unbend the knees to stand up, both palms press down, passing before the face, the chest and the abdomen with the hollows of the hands facing downward, and finally hang down naturally at the sides of the thighs. Look horizontally forward.

2. Eight Forms

As one of the main shadowboxing routines of Xingyiquan, the "Eight Forms" is also called "boxing of eight skills" for it is composed of some distinctive movements of the five-element boxing and the twelve-animal style boxing in the light of the eight methods described in ancient boxing classics as "chop, intercept, wrap, uppercut, up-stick, butt, wave and draw." This routine is well organized and smoothly linked up, with great momentum and conspicuous features of attack and defence. There is hardness as well as softness in the performance.

1) Opening Form

(1-13)

The same as those described in Fig. 1-13 of the "Five-element Linked Boxing."

2) Right Punch in Forward Step (Golden Cock Pecks at Rice)

(14-16)

The right foot takes a step forward. As you bend the right knee and shift your weight completely onto the right leg, bring the left foot next to the right ankle with the toes pointing forward. At the same time, clench both your fists. The right fist punches straight ahead with the eye of the fist on top; while the left fist presses down with the elbow bent and the forearm rotating inward until it pauses just beneath the right elbow with the centre of the fist facing downward.

Points to remember:

This is a move of active attack. You can wield your left fist to press down your opponent's on-coming hand and thrust your right fist directly at his belly. You should advance swiftly and stand on one leg firmly. Be vigorous and accurate like a cock pecking at rice.

3) Left Cannon in smooth Step (Sparrow Hawk Flies into woods)

(17-19)

The left foot takes a step forward. As you bend both knees to form a left semi-horse-riding stance, the left fist thrusts along the right fore-

arm to the front at shoulder level with the elbow slightly bent and lowered, the eye of the first on top. Meanwhile, with the forearm rotating inward, the right fist goes upward until it pauses just before the forehead, the elbow, bent, the eye of the fist at bottom and the centre of the fist facing the front. Hold the stance firm and keep your shoulders lowered. Look in the direction of the left fist.

Points to remember:

This move combines attack with defence effectively. You can raise your right arm to ward off the opponent's oncoming blow and thrust your left fist directly at his chest or face. But you should coordinate the step, the thrust and the up-block perfectly so as to exert integrated strength. With this move closely linked with the former one to make up a series of violent attack, you can leave your opponent no way of withstanding.

4) Stamp and Thrust Fist (Cannon toward Sky)

(20)

As the left foot takes half a step forward, turn your torso slightly to the right. The right fist simultaneously goes backward and downward.

(21-23)

As you turn your torso to the left, shift your weight onto the left leg. The right foot immediately goes forth and then stamps on the ground next to the left one with both knees bent. Meanwhile, open the left fist and turn the palm up. Simultaneously, the right fist continues to drop, passing beside the waist, then thrusts vigorously to the upper-front with the back of the fist brushing against the left palm. Keep both elbows slightly bent. Set your eyes on the right fist.

Points to remember:

You should first twist your torso to the right and draw the right shoulder backward so as to wield the right fist in an arc, then thrust the fist with the aid of the strength generated from the waist. You should synchronize the thrust and the stamp perfectly with a crisp sound.

5) Retreat and Draw Back (Rein Back the Horse)

(24-25)

Open the right fist. With both forearms rotating inward, two hands revolve inward round the wrists until they again get overlapped with the left palm on the back of the right hand and the hollows of the hands facing downward. Relax the wrists to ensure a smooth revolution of the hands. Set your eyes on the palms.

5

(26-27)

As the right foot takes a step backward, both palms stretch to the upper-front.

(28-30)

When you draw the left foot backward near the right one, the feet together retreat with a stamp on the ground, the knees bent and the torso inclined a little forward. At the same, both hands make a grab and pull backward and downward to the front of the abdomen, the centres of the fists facing upward.

Points to remember:

You should coordinate the pull of the hands with the retreat of the feet as though reining back

a galloping horse.

6) Right Cannon in Smooth Step (Sparrow Hawk Flies into Woods)

(31-33)

The right foot takes a step forward. The left foot immediately follows up with half a step. At the same time, the right fist thrusts forward with the elbow slightly bent and the eye of the fist on top; while the left fist drills upward, passing before the chest and the face, then, with the elbow raised and the forearm rotated inward, pauses just before the front-left of the forehead, the eye of the fist at bottom and the centre of the fist facing the front. Look straight ahead.

Points to remember:

You should advance swiftly like a spring and then hold a firm stance in order to exert great strength. You can raise your left arm to ward off the opponent's oncoming blow and thrust your right fist directly at his chest while you are stepping forward. This move embodies the imposing manner of Xingyiquan described as "Step straight ahead to strike a hard blow, leaving the enemy no way of withstanding."

7) Series Punches in Forward Step (Break through Three Passes Alone)

(34)

The left fist drops, passing beside the waist, then punches to the front with the eye of the fist on top. At the same time, the right fist withdraws to the right side of the waist with the centre of the fist facing upward.

(35-36)

The left foot takes a step forward. At the same time, the right fist punches to the front with the eye of the fist on top; while the left fist withdraws to the left side of the waist with the centre of the fist facing upward.

(37)

As you shift your weight completely onto the left leg, the right leg rises and kicks forward with the foot hooked and force concentrated on the heel. At the same time, the left fist punches to the front with the eye of the fist on top; while the right fist withdraws to the right side of the waist with the centre of the fist facing upward.

(38)

As the right foot lands to the front with your weight mainly on the left leg, the right fist punches to the front with the eye of the fist on top; while the left fist withdraws to the left side of the waist with the centre of the fist facing upward. Look straight ahead.

Points to remember:

You should carry out the step, the kick and the series punches swiftly, coordinately and continuously without any interruption, displaying an indomitable spirit. The arms must move closely against the flanks with the waist twisting correspondingly to assist the punches.

5

8) Retreat and Hold Fist against Abdomen (White Crane Spreads Wings)

(39)

As you turn your torso to the left with the toes of the left foot swung outward and those of the right foot inward to form a left bow stance, the left fist stretches to the front of the abdomen. At the same time, with the elbow, bent and the forearm rotated inward, the right fist comes back and then plunges down from outside the left forearm. Both forearms thus get crossed against the abdomen with the centres of the fists facing backward. Look to the front-left.

(40-42)

Turn your torso to the right and shift your weight onto the right leg to form a right bow stance. At the same time, raise both your fists to the upper-front of the head, and then separate them. Eyes follow the right fist.

(43-45)

The left foot takes half a step backward. When the weight is shifted beyond the left leg, both feet together retreat with a stamp, the knees bent on landing. At the same time, both fists drop from the sides, drawing a semi-circle respectively until they get together in front of the abdomen with the back of the right fist placed on the left palm and the forearms closely against the body.

Points to remember:

You should coordinate the plunge of the right fist with the left turn of the torso and the formation of the left bow stance. Then, you should synchronize the fist-holding and the retreat and stamp, exhaling with a sound to promote strength exertion. Keep the abdomen solidified with the vital energy flowing down to "dantian."

9) Jump to Left Cannon in Smooth Stance

(46-47)

As you turn the body about 130 degrees to the right with a jump and form a left semi-horse-riding stance on landing, the left palm changes into a fist and thrusts to the left side with the eye of the fist on top; while the right fist goes upward, pausing just before and above the forehead with the arm raised, the elbow bent, and the centre of the fist facing outward.

Points to remember:

You should keep your balance while jumping, and complete the up-block of the right arm and the thrust of the left fist precisely at the moment the feet land to form the semi-horse-riding stance. As you turn your torso slightly to the left.

10) Right Drill in forward Step (Sparrow Hawk Soars into Sky)

(48-50)

The right foot takes a big step forward. The left foot immediately follows up with half a step to form a left three-in-one stance. At the same

time, with the elbow bent and the forearm rotating inward, the left fist presses down, pausing just before the abdomen with the centre of the fist facing downward; while the right fist first drops to the right side of the waist, then rises, passing before the chest and the chin, and finally drills from above the left wrist to the front, the centre of the fist facing obliquely upward, the second joint of the little finger in a straight line

just before the tip of the nose.

Points to remember:

You should advance swiftly and with great momentum. The press of the left fist must be full of wrapping strength, and the drill of the right fist must coincide with the landing of the right foot.

5

11) Left Drill Turn

(51-52)

Turn your torso round to the left with the toes of the left foot swung outward and those of the right foot inward, keeping your weight mainly on the right leg. Along with the turn of the body, the right arm sweeps horizontally round.

(53-54)

Without any pause, the left foot take a step forward. The right foot immediately follows up with half a step to form a left three-in-one stance again. At the same time, with the elbow bent and the forearm rotating inward, the right fist presses down, pausing just before the abdomen with the centre of the fist facing downward; while the left fist rises with the centre of the fist turned up, and then drills from above the right wrist to the front at nose level, the elbow slightly bent and the centre of the fist facing obliquely upward. Look straight ahead.

Points to remember:

You should coordinate the sweep of the right arm with the turn of the body. Hold the fist tight and keep the elbow slightly bent while the arm sweeps round.then, you should step forward and thrust the left fist out swiftly and with great momentum.

12) Stick Up Fist (Sparrow Hawk Flips Over)

(55)

As you shift your weight slightly to the left leg, the left fist goes close to the chest with the elbow bent and the forearm rotated inward; while the right fist rises from outside the left elbow with the eye of the fist on top.

(56-57)

Turn your torso to the right and shift your weight onto the right leg. At the same time, the right fist continues to rise, pausing just before the forehead with the elbow raised and the centre of the fist facing outward; while the left fist continues to stretch down along the inner side of the left leg with the eye of the fist facing inward.

(58)

When the left fist goes past the left knee, turn your torso swiftly to the left and shift your weight a little to the left leg with both knees further bent to form a left semi-horse-riding stance. The left fist then continues to stretch forward and stick up abruptly and vigorously, the arm rotated out, the elbow slightly bent and the eye of the fist on top. In the meantime, the right fist drops to the right side of the waist with the centre of the fist facing upward. Look to the front-left.

Points to remember:

The movements of the arms should be in good harmony with the shift of the weight, the turn of the torso and the transform of the stances. You should carry out this form continuously without any interruption. The waist must be full of twisting strength while the torso turns, and the arms must be full of out-pushing strength.

Those are the description of a round of the "eight forms". You can now practise the above movements all over again, starting with the right foot taking a step forward to initiate the "Right Punch in Forward Step."

13) Closing Form

As you draw the left foot next to the right one to rise, open both your fists and raise the arms sideways with the hollows of the hands facing upward, and then move the hands inward with the elbows bent. As you slowly unbend the knees to stand up, both palms press down, passing before the face, the chest and the abdomen with the hollows of the hands facing downward, and finally hang down naturally to the sides of the thighs. Look horizontally forward.

5

3. Twelve Crosscut Punches

The "Twelve Crosscut Punches" is an advanced routine of Xingyiquan, popular mainly in Hebei and Shandong. Composed of carefully chosen skills from the five-element boxing and the twelve-animal style boxing, it has rich contents, ingenious structure, distinc- tive features of attack and defence and lively rhythm of movements. With hardness and softness supplementing each other, the perfor- mance may seem as vigorous as a tiger dash- ing down a mountain, or as supple as floating clouds and flowing water, or as nimble as a swallow flying through the woods or as graceful and vivid as a butterfly fluttering about among the flowers.

1) Opening Form

(1-13)

The same as those described in Fig. 1-13 of the "Five- element Linked Boxing."

2) Right Punch in Forward Step (Golden Cock Pecks at Rice)

(14-16)

The right foot takes a big step forward. At the same time, clench both your fists. The right fist rises from the right side of the waist to the front of the chest; while the left fist presses down- ward with the elbow bent and the forearm rotat-

ing inward.

(17-18)

As you bend the right knee and shift your weight completely onto the right leg, bring the left foot next to the right ankle with the toes pointing forward. At the same time, the right fist punches to the lower-front with the eye of the

fist on top; while the left fist moves a little back, pausing just beneath the right elbow with the centre of the fist facing downward. Look straight ahead.

Points to remember:

You should advance swiftly and stand on one leg firmly, and coordinate the punch of the right

fist with the landing of the right foot. Be vigorous and accurate like a cock pecking at rice.

3) Left Cannon in Smooth Step (Sparrow Hawk Flies into Woods)

(19-20)

The left foot takes a step forward. As you bend knees to form a left semi-horse-riding stance, the left fist thrusts along the right forearm to the front at shoulder level with the elbow slightly bent and lowered, the eye of the fist on top. Meanwhile, with the forearm rotating inward, the right fist goes upward until it pauses just before the forehead with the elbow bent, the eye of the

5

133

fist at bottom and the centre of the fist facing the front. Look in the direction of the left fist.

Points to remember:

The punch of the left fist should be in good harmony with the step of the left foot and the up-block of the right arm so as to exert integrated strength. Hold the stance firm and keep your shoulders lowered.

4) Stand on Right Leg and Hold Arms Rounded (Embrace the Moon in the Arms)

(21-22)

As you turn your torso slightly to the right

and shift your weight toward the right leg, open both your fists.

(23)

As you shift your weight completely onto the right leg with the knee slightly bent, turn your torso back to the left and raise the left leg with the knee bent, the lower leg swung inward and the foot hooked. At the same time, the left palm

moves in a horizontal arc to the front of the body at shoulder level with the elbow bent and the forearm rotated inward; while the right palm moves to the right, then drops and cuts to the front of the abdomen. You thus round the arms with the hollows of the hands facing each other as though holding a big ball in front of the body. Look to the front-right.

134

<table>
<tr><td>29</td><td>30</td><td>31</td><td>32</td></tr>
</table>

Points to remember:

You should turn your torso first to the right and then to the left with great twisting strength but without any interruption. The embrace of the arms should coincide with the raise of the left leg. Be sure to stand firm and exert closing strength through your arms.

5) Right Crosscut after Left Turn (Butterfly Flutters through Flowers)

(24-27)

After you turn about 180 degrees to the left on the ball of the right foot, the left foot takes a big step forward. At the same time, clench both your fists. The left fist moves downward and backward passing beside the waist, then swings from the side to the front; while the right fist withdraws to the right side of the waist.

(28-30)

Without any pause, the right foot takes a step forward to form a right three-in-one stance. At the same time, with the elbow bent and the forearm rotating inward, the left fist presses down to the front of the abdomen with the centre of the fist facing downward; while the right fist crosscuts from beneath the left elbow to the front with the elbow slightly bent, the centre of the fist fac-

ing obliquely upward, and the second joint of the little finger in a straight line just before the tip of the nose. Look straight ahead.

Points to remember:

You should swing the left fist in harmony with the turn of the body, and then carry out the press and the crosscut without any interruption. The crosscut is such as sweeping a bit outward with great horizontal force while the fist thrusts forward. You should finish the performance with the right shoulder pushing forth, the elbows lowered and the vital energy flowing down to "dantian."

6) Right Crosscut after Left Turn (Butterfly Flutters through Flowers)

(31-33)

Shift your weight onto the right leg and bring the left foot close to the right one as you turn about 180 degrees to the left. The left foot then takes a step forward. At the same time, the left fist moves backward passing beside the waist, then swings from the side to the front; while the right fist withdraws to the right side of the waist.

5

(34-37)

Without any pause, the right foot takes a step forward to form a right three-in-one stance. At the same time, with the elbow bent and the forearm rotating inward, the left fist presses down to the front of the abdomen with the centre of the fist facing downward; while the right fist crosscuts from beneath the left elbow to the front with the elbow slightly bent, the centre of the fist facing obliquely upward and the second joint of the little finger in a straight line just before the tip of the nose. Look straight ahead.

Points to remember:

The same as those of the Form 5.

7) Stand on Left Leg and Hold Arms Rounded (Embrace the Moon in the Arms)

(38-40)

As you turn your torso first slightly to the left and then back to the right, shift your weight completely onto the left leg with the knee slightly bent, and raise the right leg with the knee bent, the lower leg swung inward and the foot hooked. At the same time, open both your fists. The right palm moves to the front of the body at shoulder level with the elbow bent and the forearm rotated inward; while the left palm moves a little backward and then cuts to the front of the abdomen. You thus round the arms with the hollows of the hands facing each other as though

136

holding a big ball in front of the body. Look to the front-left.

Points to remember:
The same as those of the Form 4.

8) Left Crosscut after Right Turn (Butterfly Flutters through Flowers)

(41-43)
After you turn about 180 degrees to the right on the ball of the left foot, the right foot takes a big step forward. At the same time, clench both your fists. The right fist moves downward and backward passing beside the waist, then swings from the side to the front; while the left fist withdraws to the left side of the waist.

(44-45)
Without any pause, the left foot takes a step forward to form a left three-in-one stance. At the same time, with the elbow bent and the forearm rotating inward, the right fist presses down to the front of the abdomen with the centre of the fist facing downward; while the left fist crosscuts from beneath the right elbow to the front with the elbow slightly bent, the centre of the fist facing obliquely upward and the second

joint of the little finger in a straight line just before the tip of the nose. Look straight ahead.

Points to remember:
The same as those of the Form 5, only with "left" and "right" reversed.

5

9) Left Crosscut after Right Turn (Butterfly Flutters through Flowers)

(46-48)

Shift your weight onto the left leg and bring the right foot close to the left one as you turn about 180 degrees to the right. The right foot then takes a step forward. At the same time, the fist moves backward passing beside the waist, then swings from the side to the front; while the left fist withdraws to the left side of the waist.

(49-52)

Without any pause, the left foot takes a step

forward to form a left three-in-one stance. At the same time, with the elbow bent and the forearm rotating inward, the right fist presses down to the front of the abdomen with the centre of the fist facing downward; while the left fist crosscuts from beneath the right elbow to the front with the elbow slightly bent, the centre of the fist facing obliquely upward and the second joint of the little finger in a straight line just before the tip of the nose. Look straight ahead.

Points to remember:

The same as those of the Form 5, only with "left" and "right" reversed.

138

10) Right Punch in Forward Step (Black Tiger Enters Lair)

(53-56)

The left foot takes a big step forward. The right foot immediately follows up with half a step to form a left three-in-one stance. At the same time, the right fist punches straight ahead with the elbow slightly bent and the eye of the fist on top; while the left fist withdraws to the left side of the waist with the centre of the fist facing upward.

Points to remember:

Step forwards swiftly and then take a firm stance. When the right fist thrusts forward, you should twist the torso to the left with the right shoulder pushing forth to exert piercing strength.

11) Left Punch in Forward Step (Black Tiger Enters Lair)

(57-58)

The left foot takes a big step forward. The right foot immediately follows up with half a step to form a left three-in-one stance. At the same time, the left fist punches straight ahead with the elbow slightly bent and the eye of the fist on top; while the right fist withdraws to the right side of the waist with the center of the fist facing upward. Look straight ahead.

Points to remember:

The same as those of the Form10, only with "left" and "right" reversed.

5

12) Dash with Both Palms in Round Step (Two Tigers Grapple)

(59-60)

As you turn your torso slightly to the left and shift your weight onto the right leg, bring the left foot close to the right one. At the same time, both fists move to the front of the abdomen and get crossed with the left arm in and the right arm out, the centres of the fists facing backward.

(61)

As the left foot continues to step to the front along curve, both fists change into palms and rise to the front of the face.

(62-63)

As you turn about 45 degrees to the left on the ball of the left foot, the right foot goes forth with the knee bent. At the same time, both palms separate, and then drop to the sides of the waist with the fingers pointing downward and the hollows of the hands facing the front.

(64-67)

The right foot continues to stride forward. The left foot immediately follows up with half a step to form a right three-in-one stance with the weight mainly on the left leg. At the same time, both palms

140

dash straight ahead at abdomen level with the elbows slightly bent, the bases of the palms about 15 cm apart and the fingers pointing to the lower-front.

Points to remember:

The left foot should move in an arc and with a giant stride. Both arms should circle smoothly and in harmony with the turn of the body and the step of the left foot. You should coordinate the dash of the palms with the stride of the right foot, making full use of the impulsive force generated along with the stride.

13) Turn and Dash with Both Palms (Hungry Tiger Pounces on Its prey)

(68-71)

As you turn round to the left with the toes of the right foot swung inward, raise the left leg with the knee bent and the foot close to the right ankle. At the same time, both palms drop to the sides, and then continue to swing sideways to shoulder level with the elbow bent and the hollows of the hands turned up.

(72-73)

As you continue to turn to the left with the toes of the left foot resting on the ground, both palms press from beside the ears to the front of

the chest with the elbows further bent and the hollows of the hands turned down.

(74-76)

Without any pause, the left foot takes a step forward. The right foot immediately follows up with half a step to form a left three-in-one stance. At the same time, both palms dash to the front at shoulder level with the elbows slightly bent, the arches between the thumb and the forefinger facing each other, and the hollows of the hands facing forward. Look straight ahead.

Points to remember:

Both arms should swing smoothly and continuously without any interruption, and in good harmony with the turn of about 270 degrees in all. You should step forward swiftly and carry out the dash like a hungry tiger pouncing on its prey.

5

14) Thrust Palm Downward in a Squat (Golden Cock Perches on High Frame)

(77-79)

The right foot takes a step forward. At the same time, the right arm moves backward with the elbow bent and the hollow of the hand facing downward; while the left palm rises, and then thrusts downward from before the chest with the fingers leading the way.

(80-81)

As you bend the right knee to squat yourself

down, bring the left foot forward and place its toes emptily on the ground next to the right foot. At the same time, the left palm continues to thrusts down to the front of the right knee with the hollow of the hand facing the left and the fingers pointing downward; while the right palm swings to the front of the left cheek with the hollow of the hand facing the left and the fin-

gers pointing upward. Look straight ahead.

Points to remember:

The right foot should go forth with a giant stride and a steady landing. You should then squat down and bring the left foot forward swiftly without any interruption. Keep your breast slightly in so as to store up strength for exertion at any time.

15) Swing Left Palm in Forward Step (Golden Cock Crows at Dawn)

(82-84)

With a powerful drive of the right foot to push the body up, the left foot takes a big step forward. The right foot immediately follows up with half a step to form a left three-in-one stance. At the same, the left palm swings forward and upward to shoulder level with the elbow slightly bent, the thumb side of the hand on top; while the right palm presses down to the side of the right hip with the hollow of the hand facing downward. Look straight ahead.

Points to remember:

The left foot should go forth swiftly, and push forward on landing to keep a firm stance. You should take advantage of the rise of the body to swing the left palm forward and upward, and synchronize the swing with the press of the right palm and the step of the left foot.

16) Right Drill in Forward Step (Sparrow Hawk Soars into Sky)

(85-88)

After the left foot goes a little forth, the right foot takes a step forward. The left foot immediately follows up with half a step to form a left three-in-one stance. At the same time, with the elbow bent and the forearm rotating inward, the left palm presses down, pausing just before the abdomen with the palm changed into a fist and the centre of the fist facing downward; while the right palm changes into a fist and rises passing before the chest and the chin, and finally drills from above the left wrist to the front at nose level with the elbow slightly bent and the centre of the fist facing obliquely upward. Look straight ahead.

Points to remember:

The drill of the right fist should be full of spring force and coincide with the swift step of the right foot. Keep your shoulders lowered and your abdomen solidified with the vital energy flowing down to "dantian."

5

17) Left Drill after Turn (Sparrow Hawk Soars into Sky)

(89-90)

Turn Your torso round to the left with the toes of the left foot swung outward and those of the right one inward. Then, shift your weight onto the right leg and raise the left foot with the knee bent. Along with the turn of the body, the right arm sweeps horizontally round.

(91-92)

Without any pause, the left foot takes a step forward. The right foot immediately follows up with half a step to form a left three-in-one stance again. At the same time, with the elbow bent and the forearm rotating inward, the right fist presses down, pausing just before the abdomen with the centre of the fist facing downward; while the left fist rises, passing before the chest and the chin with the centre of the fist turned up, and then drills from above the right wrist to the front with the elbow slightly bent, the centre of the fist facing obliquely upward, and the second joint of the little finger in a straight line just before the tip of the nose. Look straight ahead.

Points to remember:

You should tighten your right shoulder and coordinate the sweep of the right arm with the turn of the body so as to exert great horizontal force. After the turn, the step of the left foot and the thrust of the left fist must be completed simultaneously.

18) Stick Up fist (Sparrow Hawk Flips Over)

(93-94)

Shift your weight slightly to the left leg. Then, turn your torso to the right and shift your weight back to the right leg. At the same time, the left fist goes close to the chest with the elbow bent and the forearm rotated inward; while the right fist rises from outside the left elbow, pausing just before the forehead with the elbow raised and the centre of the fist facing outward.

(95-97)

As you bend the knees further to lower the body, the left fist continues to stretch down along the inner side of the left leg. When the left fist goes past the left knee, turn your torso swiftly to the left and shift your weight a little to the left leg to form a left semi-horse-riding stance. The left fist then continues to stretch forward and stick up abruptly and vigorously, the arm rotated outward, the elbow slightly bent and the eye of the fist on top. In the meantime, the right fist drops to the right side of the waist with the centre of the fist facing upward. Look to the front-left.

Points to remember:

The movements of the arms should be in good harmony with the shift of the weight, the turn of the torso and the transform of the stances. You should carry out this form continuously without any interruption. The waist must be full of twisting strength while the torso turns, and the arms must be full of out-pushing strength.

19) Right Punch in Forward Step (Golden Cock Pecks at Rice)

(98-102)

The same as those described in Fig. 14-18, except that you are now performing the other

way round.

20) Left Cannon in Smooth Step (Sparrow Hawk Flies into Woods)

(103-104)

The same as those described in Fig. 19-20, except that you are now performing the other way round.

145

except that you are now performing the other way round.

21) Stand on Right Leg and Hold Arms Rounded (Embrace the Moon in the Arms)

(105-108)

The same as those described in Fig. 21-23,

22) Right Crosscut after Left Turn (Butterfly Flutters through Flowers)

(109-114)

The same as those described in Fig. 24-30, except that you are now performing the other way round.

23) Right Crosscut after Left Turn (Butterfly Flutters through Flowers)

way round.

(115-122)

The same as those described in Fig. 31-37, except that you are now performing the other

way round.

24) Stand on Left Leg and Hold Arms Rounded (Embrace the Moon in the Arms)

(123-126)

The same as those described in Fig. 38-40, except that you are now performing the other

5

25) Left Crosscut after Right Turn (Butterfly Flutters through Flowers)

(127-132)

The same as those described in Fig. 41-45, except that you are now performing the other way round.

26) Left Crosscut after Right Turn (Butterfly Flutters through Flowers)

(133-138)

The same as those described in Fig. 46-52, except that you are now performing the other way round.

27) Right Punch in Forward Step (Black Tiger Enters Lair)

(139-141)

The same as those described in Fig. 53-56, except that you are now performing the other way round.

28) Left Punch in Forward Step (Black Tiger Enters Lair)

5

(142-145)

The same as those described in Fig. 57-58, except that you are now performing the other way round.

29) Dash with Both Palms in Round Step (Two Tigers Grapple)

(146-153)

The same as those described in Fig. 59-67, except that you are now performing the other way round.

30) Turn and Dash with Both Palms (Hungry Tiger Pounces on Its Prey)

(154-161)

The same as those described in Fig. 68-76, ex-cept that you are now performing the other way round.

31) Thrust Palm Downward in a Squat (Golden Cock Perch on High Frame)

(162-166)

The same as those described in Fig. 77-81, except that you are now performing the other way round.

5

32) Swing Left Palm in Forward Step (Golden Cock Crows at Dawn)

(167-170)

The same as those described in Fig. 82-84, except that you are now performing the other way round.

33) Right Drill in Forward Step (Sparrow Hawk Soars into Sky)

(171-175)

The same as those described in Fig. 85-88, except that you are now performing the other way round.

152

34) Left Drill after Turn (Sparrow Hawk Soars into Sky)

(176-180)

The same as those described in Fig. 89-92, except that you are now performing the other way round.

5

35) Stick Up Fist (Sparrow Hawk Flips Over)

(181-185)

The same as those described in Fig. 93-97, except that you are now performing the other way round.

153

36) Right Punch in Forward Step
(Golden Cock Pecks at Rice)

(186-190)

The same as those described in Fig. 14-18.

154

37) Left Cannon in Smooth Step (Sparrow Hawk Flies into Woods)

(19-193)

The same as those described in Fig. 19-20.

38) Right Crosscut after Left Turn (Butterfly Flutters through Flowers)

(194-201)

The same as those described in Fig. 24-30.

5

155

39) Wag the Body and Strike Fists Down (Ram the Earth and Shake the Mountains)

(202-203)

Shift your weight onto the right leg. Bring the left foot next to the right one with the toes touching the ground, and then move it a little outward. At the same time, the right fist moves to the front of the chest with the elbow bent; while the left fist drills upward from outside the right elbow. Set your eyes on the right fist.

(204-205)

The left foot takes a step to the side with the heel first touching the ground. As you turn your torso to the left, both forearms get crossed in front of the chest with the right one in and the left one out. The forearms then revolve inward round the elbows.

(206-208)

As you shift your weight a little forward and bend both knees to form a left semi-horse-riding stance, the fists respectively strike down to the front of the crotch with the elbows slightly bent, the right fist at knee level and the left one a little lower than the knees. Hold the fists tight with the centres of the fists facing backward, the

forefist of the right one facing obliquely downward and that of the left fist directly facing the ground.

Points to remember:

Keep your breast slightly in and the forearms clinging to each other while you revolve the fists in front of the chest. You should strike the fists down with great explosive force that is generated from the waist, transmitted to the shoulders and finally brought to the forefists. Hold the stance firm with the vital energy flowing down to "dantian."

ward; while the left fist rises to the front of the chest. Look straight ahead.

40) The Three-in-one Posture

(209-211)

As you turn your torso slightly to the left, the right fist goes upward, passing before the chest and the chin, then changes into a palm and reaches to the front with the elbow slightly bent and the hollow of the hand facing obliquely for-

5

(212-214)

Without any pause, the left fist changes into a palm and chops from before the chin to the front at shoulder level, the hollow of the hand facing the lower-front, the forefinger pointing upward and the thumb stretching extremely outward; while the right palm withdraws until the root of the thumb gets close against the abdomen with the wrist lowered, the forefinger tilting slightly upward and the hollow of the hand facing downward. Look in the direction of the left palm.

Points to remember:

You should carry out this form slowly, steadily and continuously, with your attention concentrated and your vital energy stored up.

41) Closing Form

(215)

As you turn your torso to the right with the toes of the left foot swung inward, the right arm swings sideward and upward. Rotate both the arms outward in the meantime. Eyes follow the right palm.

(216-217)

Turn your torso slightly to the left with the toes of the right foot swung slightly inward, and bring the left foot next to the right one with the heels together and the toes of the feet pointing obliquely outward. At the same time, both palms continue to move upward and inward with the elbows bent and the hollows of the hands turned down.

(218-220)

As you slowly unbend the knees to stand up, both palms press down from before the face to the front of the abdomen with the hollows of the hands facing downward and the fingers of two hands pointing to each other.

(221)

Stand upright with the arms hanging down naturally at the sides of the thighs. Look horizontally forward.

Points to remember:

At the beginning of this form, you should turn your torso to the right and swing the right arm out slowly. Then, you ought to speed up the pace slightly while you draw back the left foot and move the palms inward. Finally, you should perform the press of the palms in good harmony with the straightening of the legs and in a gentle manner. Be sure to concentrate your attention and relax the whole body.

5

6

Chapter Six

Paired Practice

1. Five-element Cannon

The Five- element Cannon is a wide-spread sparring routine formerly called "the mutual restraint of the five elements". It was created on the ancient concept of the five elements, metal, wood, water, fire and earth. It was believed that metal could restrain wood, wood could restrain earth, earth could restrain water, water could restrain fire and fire could restrain metal. As the basic methods of Xingyiquan, chop, drill, punch, cannon and crosscut respectively represent the five elements, therefore come the corresponding relationships between the boxing methods: chop suppresses punch, punch suppresses crosscut, crosscut suppresses drill, drill suppresses cannon and cannon suppresses chop.

Through constant exercise with this sparring routine, you can not only heighten your consciousness of attack and defence, deepen your comprehension of the practical skills of the five-element boxing, but also improve your nimbleness and harmoniousness. Usually, you can perform the 9 forms for two rounds and then finish up with the closing form. If your physical condition permits, you can also practise again and again until you want to rest.

1) Preparatory Form

Both A (on the left) and B (on the right) take a left three-in-one posture respectively, facing each other with the front hands about 10 to 20 centimeters apart. (Fig. 1)

2)

A: Right Punch in Forward Step
The left foot goes forth with a quick and giant stride. The right foot immediately follows up with half a step to form a left three-in-one stance. At the same time, clench both

the fists. The right fist thus punches vigorously toward B's belly; while the left fist withdraws to the left side of the waist. (Fig. 2-4)

B: Left Press in Retreat Step
The right foot moves backward swiftly. The left foot immediately retreats next to the right one with the toes resting on the ground. At the same time, the left hand presses A's right forearm down to ward off the blow. (Fig. 2-4)

3)

A: Left Punch in Forward Step
The left foot goes forth. The right foot immediately follows up with half a step to form a left three-in-one stance. At the same time, the left fist punches vigorously toward B's belly; while the right fist withdraws to the right side of the waist. (Fig. 5-6)

B: Right Chop in Round Step
The right foot moves backward swiftly. The left foot immediately retreats, bypassing A's left foot, then steps forward. At the same time, the left hand rounds counterclockwise from under A's left fist and then presses A's left wrist from the outside. The right foot then takes a step forward. Simultaneously, the right hand stretches upward and forward to chop at A's face; while the left hand withdraws to the front of the abdomen. (Fig. 5-7)

4)

A: Right Cannon in Retreat Step
The left foot takes a step to the rear. At the same time, the left arm rises with the elbow bent to ward off B's right palm; while the right fist thrusts straight into B's chest. (Fig. 7-8)

B: Left Drill in Forward Step
The right hand presses down to pluck aside A's right fist. The left foot then takes a step forward. As the left foot goes forth, the left hand changes into a fist and drills swiftly into A's throat. The right hand withdraws to the right side of the waist in the meantime. (Fig. 8-11)

5)

A: Left Crosscut in Retreat Step

As the right foot swiftly takes a step to the rear, the left fist crosscuts to the upper-front to ward off B's left fist. The right fist withdraws to the front of the abdomen in the meantime. (Fig. 9-12)

6)

B: Right Punch in Forward Step

The left foot goes forth. The right foot immediately follows up with half a step to form a left three-in-one stance. At the same time, the right fist punches straight toward A's belly; while the left fist withdraws to the left side of the waist. (Fig. 12-15)

A: Left Press in Retreat Step

The right foot moves backward quickly. The left foot immediately retreats close to the right one. At the same time, the left hand presses B's right forearm down to ward off the blow. (Fig. 13-15)

7)

B: Left Punch in Forward Step

The left foot goes forth. The right foot immediately follows up with half a step to form a left three-in-one stance. At the same time, the left fist punches vigorously toward A's belly; while the right fist withdraws to the right side of the waist. (Fig. 16-17)

A: Right Chop in Round Step

The right foot moves backward swiftly. The left foot immediately retreats, bypassing B's left foot, then steps forward. At the same time, the left hand rounds counterclockwise from under B's left fist and then presses B's left wrist from the outside. The right foot then takes a step forward. The right fist simultaneously changes into a palm and stretches upward and forward to chop at B's face; while the left hand withdraws to the front of the abdomen. (Fig. 16-19)

8)

B: Right Cannon in Retreat Step

The left foot takes a step to the rear. At the same time, the left arm rises with the elbow bent to ward off A's right palm; while the right fist thrusts straight into A's chest (Fig. 18-20)

A: Left Drill in Forward Step

The right hand presses down to pluck aside B's right fist. The left foot then takes a step forward. As the left foot goes forth, the left hand changes into a fist and drills swiftly into B's throat. The right hand withdraws to the right side of the waist in the meantime. (Fig. 20-23)

9)

B: Left Crosscut in Retreat Step

As the right foot swiftly takes a step to the rear, the left fist crosscut to the front to ward off A's left fist. The right fist withdraws to the front of the abdomen in the meantime. (Fig. 21-23)

10) Closing Form

The right fist stretches forward to shoulder level. Then, bring the left foot next to the right one and unbend both knees to stand upright. Both arms drop to the sides of the body with the fists opened in the meantime. Look horizontally at each other.

6

2. Body-guarding Cannon

The Body-guarding Cannon is an advanced sparring routine of Xingyiquan. As a collection of choice skills of the five-element boxing and the twelve-animal style boxing, it is well organized, rich in content and much more complicated, exhibiting such features of Xingyiquan as having hardness and softness promoting each other, fighting with compact and intensive skills at close quarters, exerting great strength and being simple but practical. Practitioners should try to grasp the key points of every form, master the essence of every method, cooperate well with the partner and take the offensive and the defensive in due rhythm without any slackness.

Constant exercise with the Body-guarding Cannon can not only bring benefit to your eyes, limbs and trunk, but also increase the reaction effectiveness and the flexibility of your nervous system, therefore help you to master the attack and defence methods of Xingyiquan and enhance your capacity of self-defence.

1) Preparatory Form

Both **A** (on the left) and **B** (on the right) take a left three-in-one posture respectively, facing each other with the front hands about 10 to 20 centimeters apart. (Fig. 1)

2)

A: Right Punch in Forward Step

The left foot goes forth with a giant stride. The right foot immediately follows up with half a step to form a left three-in-one stance. At the same time, clench both the fists. The right fist thus punches violently toward **B**'s belly; while the left fist withdraws to the left side of the waist. (Fig. 2-4)

B: Left Push and right Punch

As the weight is shifted backward and the left leg is lifted with the knee bent, the left hand catches hold of **A**'s right wrist and pushes the arm to the

right. Then, the left foot steps forward. The right foot immediately follows up with half a step to form a left three-in-one stance. At the same time, the right hand changes into a fist and punches toward **A**'s belly; while the left hand changes into a fist and withdraws to the left side of the waist. (Fig. 2-6)

3)

A: Left Chop

As the right hand presses down upon **B**'s right fist to ward off the blow, the left fist changes into a palm and stretches forward to chop at **B**'s right arm. (Fig. 5-6)

B: Left Cannon

As the right arm rises with the elbow bent to block **A**'s left palm, the left fist thrusts straight into **A**'s chest. (Fig. 7-8)

4)

A: Right Chop in Round Step

As the left foot rounds to the outside of **B**'s left foot, the left hand rounds counterclockwise from under **B**'s left fist. The right foot then takes a step forward. At the same time, the right hand goes up, then chops at **B**'s face. The left hand simultaneously presses **B**'s left fist down and then withdraws to the front of the abdomen. (Fig. 7-12)

6

B: Left Parry and Right Horizontal Slap

The left foot swiftly takes a step to the rear. At the same time, the left hand swings upward and then moves outward and downward to pluck aside **A**'s right arm; while the right fist changes into a palm and swings from the side horizontally to the front to slap **A** on the left ear. (Fig. 9-14)

5)

A: Left Double Interception

Hold both arms in front of the chest with the elbows bent and the palms changed into fists. As the torso swiftly twists to the left, both arms sway to the left to intercept **B**'s right forearm. (Fig. 13-15)

B: Left Horizontal Slap

The left hand swings from the side horizontally to the front to slap **A** on the right ear. The right hand withdraws to the right side of the waist in the meantime. (Fig. 15-16)

6)

A: Right Double Interception and Right Punch

As the torso swiftly twists to the right, both arms sway to the right to intercept **B**'s left forearm. After that, the right fist goes down and punches toward **B**'s belly; while the left fist withdraws to the left side of the waist. (Fig. 16-18)

6

B: Double Uplift and Right Punch

As the weight is shifted backward, the right hand catches hold of **A**'s right fist from the bottom and lifts it. Then, the left hand takes over to lift **A**'s right fist; while the right hand changes into a fist and drops to the right side of the waist. After that, as the weight is shifted forward, the right fist punches toward **A**'s belly; while the left hand withdraws to the left side of the waist. (Fig. 17-21)

7)

A: Double Press and Right Chop

As the weight is swiftly shifted backward, the right hand and the left hand successively press **B**'s right arm down. Then, as the weight is shifted forward, the right hand goes up to chop at **B**'s face. (Fig. 19-23)

6

B: Left Press and Right Drill

As the weight is shifted a little backward, the left hand rises and then presses **A**'s right wrist down. Then, as the weight is shifted forward, the right fist drills toward **A**'s face. (Fig. 22-26)

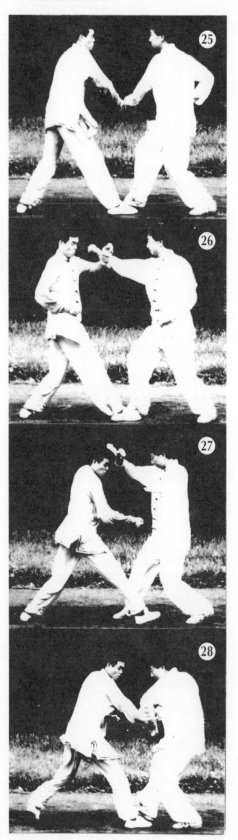

8)

A: Left Crosscut and Right Punch

As the torso swiftly twists to the right, clench both the fists. The left fist thus crosscuts to the upper-front to ward off **B**'s right fist. Then, as the right foot goes forth and the torso twists to the left, the right fist punches from beside the waist toward **B**'s belly. (Fig.26-27)

B: Left Press in Retreat Step

The right foot moves backward swiftly. As the torso turns to the right, the left foot retreats next to the right one with the toes resting on the ground. At the same time, the left hand presses **A**'s right wrist down; while the right hand withdraws to the right side of the waist. (Fig. 27-30)

6

9)

A: Left Press and Right Horizontal Slap

The left hand reaches forward to pluck aside **B**'s left arm. Then, as the right foot goés forth, the right hand changes into a palm and swings from the side horizontally to the front to slap **B** on the left ear. (Fig. 31-33)

B: Left Parry in Retreat Step

The right foot moves backward. At the same time, the left hand swings upward to head level with the elbow bent to parry **A**'s right palm. The left foot then retreats next to the right one. (Fig. 31-34)

10)

A: Left Press and Right Horizontal Slap
The left hand stretches forward from under the right arm and then presses down upon **B**'s right wrist. As the right foot then goes forth, the right hand moves a little back, then swings from the side horizontally to the front to slap **B** on the left ear. (Fig. 35-36)

B: Parry, Press and Backhanded Slap
The right foot moves backward. The left foot immediately retreats next to the right one. At the same time, the left hand swings upward to head level with the elbow bent to parry **A**'s right palm. After that, the left foot goes forth with the toes turned outward. The right foot immediately takes a step forward. As the body turns to the left with the weight shifted forward, the left hand presses **A**'s right arm down. Meanwhile, the right hand stretches forward to press **A**'s right upper arm, then whips forth to slap **A** backhanded on the right ear. (Fig. 35-39)

6

11)

A: Left Chop in Round Step

The right foot moves a little backward, bypassing B's right foot, then steps forward with the toes turned outward. The left foot immediately takes a step to the outside of B's right foot. At the same time, the right hand rounds clockwise from under B'd right arm and then presses the forearm down; while the left hand stretches forward to chop at B's right shoulder. (Fig. 39-43)

B: Parry with Knee Lifted and Right Chop

As the right leg is abruptly lifted with the knee bent, the right hand swiftly swings upward to parry **A**'s left palm. The left hand simultaneously rises and then presses **A**'s left arm down. After that, as the right foot steps to the front, the right hand chops at **A**'s left shoulder. (Fig. 44-45)

12)

A: Dash in Forward Step

The left hand rises with the elbow bent to block **B**'s blow and then catches hold of the wrist. At the same time, the right foot takes a step toward **B**'s right side. The body thus dashes forth with the right shoulder ramming against **B**'s torso. (Fig. 45-48)

B: Double Pull in Retreat Step

The right foot swiftly takes a step to the rear. As the weight is shifted backward, both hands catch hold of **A**'s right arm and pull it toward the right-rear. (Fig. 46-49)

6

13)

A: Left Horizontal Slap in Twisted Stance
The left hand swings from the side horizontally to the front to slap **B** on the right ear. The right hand withdraws in the meantime. (Fig. 50-51)

B: Right Drill
The right hand changes into a fist and drills to the upper-front to ward off **A**'s left arm. The left hand withdraws to the left side of the waist in the meantime. (Fig. 50-51)

14)

A: Right Horizontal Slap
The right hand swings from the side horizontally to the front to slap **B** on the left ear. The left hand withdraws in the meantime. (Fig. 52)

B: Right Interception and Left Punch

As the torso swiftly turns to the left, the right arm vigorously sways to the left with the elbow bent to intercept **A**'s right forearm. Then, as the torso turns to the right, the left hand changes into a fist and punches toward **A**'s belly. The right fist withdraws to the right side of the waist in the meantime. (Fig. 53-54)

15)

A: Double Press and Right Chop

The right hand presses **B**'s left fist down. Then, as the left hand takes over to press **B**'s left arm, the right hand stretches forward to chop at B's face. (Fig. 54-56)

B: Right Crosscut in Retreat Step

The left foot takes a step to the rear. At the same time, the right fist crosscuts to the upper-front to ward off **A**'s right palm; while the left fist withdraws to the left side of the waist. (Fig. 57-58)

16)

A: Left Block and Right Smash

As the torso turns to the right with the toes of the right foot swung outward, the left hand changes into a fist and swings upward with the elbow bent to block **B**'s right fist. Then, the left foot takes a step forward to form a left bow stance, the thigh of the leg pressing **B**'s right leg from the outside. At the same time, the right forearm smashes straight into **B**'s belly, the elbow bent, the hand changed into a fist and the force concentrated on the little finger side of the forearm. (Fig. 59-60)

B: Left Double Interception

Hold both arms in front of the chest with the elbows bent. As the torso turns to the left, the body swiftly huddles up and squats a little down. Both arms thus sway toward the lower- left to intercept **A**'s right forearm. (Fig. 61-62)

6

17)

A: Left Swat

The left fist changes into a palm and swats **B** on the right cheek, the force concentrated on the base of the palm. (Fig. 63-64)

B: Double Interception and Right Punch

As the torso swiftly twists to the right, both arms sway to the upper-right to intercept **A**'s left forearm. The right fist then drops,passing beside the waist, and continues to punch straight into **A**'s belly.The left fist withdraws to the front of the abdomen in the meantime. (Fig. 63-67)

18)

A: Left Press and Right Drill

As the torso turns to the right, shift the weight onto the right leg with the knee bent. The left foot immediately retreats next to the right one with the toes resting on the ground. At the same time, the left hand presses **B**'s right fist down; while the right fist withdraws to the right side of the waist. (Fig. 67-68) After that, as the torso turns to the left with the weight completely shifted onto the left leg, the right leg rises to tread on **B**'s right knee. The right fist simultaneously drills toward **B**'s face. (Fig. 69)

B: Right Crosscut with Knee Lifted

As the right leg is swiftly lifted with the knee bent to avoid **A**'s kick, the right fist crosscuts to the upper-front to ward off **A**'s right fist. (Fig. 69-70)

6

19)

A: Series Chops in Forward Steps

As the right foot steps forward, the right fist changes into a palm and chops down (Fig. 71-72). Then, when the left foot takes a step forward, the left hand goes up and continues to chop to the front; while the right hand withdraws to the front of the abdomen (Fig. 73-74). Without any break, as the weight is shifted forward to form a left bow stance, the right hand goes up and continues to chop at **B**'s face; while the left hand withdraws to the front of the abdomen (Fig. 75).

B: Right Crosscut in Backward Hop

As the left foot vigorously pushes off the ground to hop backward, the right fist drops to the right side of the body. After the left foot makes the landing, the right foot takes a step to the rear. At the same time, the right fist crosscuts to the upper-front to ward off **A**'s right palm. (Fig. 71-75)

20)

A: Left Parry and Right Horizontal Cut

As the weight is shifted slightly backward, the left hand swings to the upper-front to parry **B**'s right arm aside. The right hand simultaneously moves a little back with the elbow bent. Then, as the weight is shifted forward, the right hand swings forth to cut **B** at the neck, the force concentrated on the little finger side of the palm; while the left hand withdraws to the left side of the waist. (Fig. 76-79)

B: Left Grab at Shoulder

As the torso sways backward, the left hand goes up with the elbow bent to parry **A**'s right arm. Then, as the weight is swiftly shifted forward, the left hand swings forward along **A**'s right arm and makes a close grab at **A**'s right shoulder. The right fist withdraws to the right side of the body in the meantime. (Fig. 78-80)

6

21)

A: Right Pluck and Right Cut

As the torso swiftly turns to the right with the weight shifted backward and the right shoulder drawn backward, the right hand, catching hold of **B**'s left wrist from the outside with the elbow bent, and the left hand, pressing **B**'s left palm from the inside, together pluck **B**'s left arm aside. Then, as the weight is swiftly shifted forward, the right hand swings forth to cut **B** at the neck, the force concentrated on the little finger side of the palm. (Fig. 81-83)

B: Left Parry and Right Slap

As the weight is swiftly shifted backward, the left hand swings upward with the elbow bent to parry **A**'s right arm aside. Then, as the torso swiftly twists to the left, the right hand swings from the side horizontally to the front to slap **A** on the left ear, the force concentrated on the base of the palm. The left hand withdraws to the left side of the body in the meantime. (Fig. 82-84)

22)

A: Left Double Interception
Hold both arms in front of the chest with the elbows bent and the palms changed into fists. As the torso twists to the left, both arms sway to the left to intercept **B**'s right forearm. (Fig. 84)

B: Left Slap
The left hand swings from the side horizontally to the front to slap **A** on the right ear. (Fig. 85)

23)

A: Right Double Interception and Right Punch
As the torso swiftly twists to the right, both arms sway to the right to intercept B's left forearm. After that, the right fist goes down and then punches straight into **B**'s belly. The left fist withdraws to the left side of the waist in the meantime. (Fig. 85-87)

6

B: Left Push and Right Punch

As the left leg is lifted with the knee bent, the left hand makes a grab at **A**'s right wrist and pushes the fist to the right. Then, as the left foot steps forward, the right hand changes into a fist and punches straight into **A**'s belly. (Fig. 87-89)

24)

A: Left Push with Knee Lifted and Right Punch

As the left leg is lifted with the knee bent, the left hand changes into a palm and pushes **B**'s right fist to the right. Then, as the left foot steps forward, the right fist punches from beside the waist straight into **B**'s belly. (Fig. 89-91)

B: Left Chop

The right fist changes into a palm and presses **A**'s right fist down. At the same time, the left fist changes into a palm and goes up to chop at **A**'s face. (Fig. 91-92)

25)

A: Left Cannon

As the right arm rises with the elbow bent to block **B**'s left palm, the left hand changes into a fist and thrusts straight into **B**'s chest. (Fig. 93-94)

26) Closing Form

Bring the left foot next to the right one and unbend both knees to stand upright. Lower both arms to the sides of the body in the meantime. Look horizontally at each other.

If both of you do not want to stop, you can skip over the closing form and repeat all the movements from Form 4 to Form 26 only with **A** and **B** exchanged.

Martial Arts Book List

Morihei Ueshiba **Budo Training in Aikido** (Traditional Japanese hand-bind)

Morihiro Saito **Traditional Aikido**-Sword, Stick, Body Arts (Soft cover)
Contents of: **Vol. 1** Basic techniques **Vol. 2** Sword and Jo Techniques
Vol. 3 Body Techniques **Vol. 4** Varied Techniques,
Vol. 5 Training Methods

Morihiro Saito **AIKIDO** -Its Heart and Appearance (Soft cover)

Risuke Otake **The Deity and the Sword**-Katori Shinto Ryu (Soft cover)
Contents of: **Vol. 1** Iai-jutsu, Bojutsu (Staff) **Vol. 2** Sword Techniques
Vol. 3 Heiho, Two-sword, Naginata, So-jutsu (Spear)

Morio Higaonna **Traditional Karate-do**-Okinawa Goju Ryu
Vol. 1 Fundamental Techniques **Vol. 2** Performances of the Kata
Vol. 3 Applications of the Kata **Vol. 4** Applications of the Kata

PART 2

T. Watanabe **Shinkage-ryu Sword Techniques**
-Traditional Japanese Martial Arts **Vol. 1, Vol. 2**

Xing Yanling **T'ai Chi Ch'uan**-The Basic Exercises (24 Movements)

Xing Yanling **Tai-chi Swordplay and Eight-diagram Palm**

Xing Yanling **Chen Style T'ai Chi Ch'uan**-Thirty-six and Fifty-six
Movements

Cai Chuxian **Fukien Ground Boxing**-Nan Shaolin Leg Techniques

Lin Jianhua **Form and Will Boxing**-One of the Big Three Internal
Chinese Body Boxing Styles *(Shing Yee Ch'uan)*

T. Sugawara, **Aikido and Chinese Martial Arts**-A Comparative
Xing Lujian Study On Two Different but Similar Martial Arts

T. Sugawara, **Aikido and Chinese Martial Arts**-Aikido and
Xing Lujian Weapons Training
and Mark Jones